THE
RUTH
ANOINTING

MICHELLE McCLAIN-WALTERS

CHARISMA
HOUSE

Most CHARISMA HOUSE BOOK GROUP products are available at special quantity discounts for bulk purchase for sales promotions, premiums, fund-raising, and educational needs. For details, write Charisma House Book Group, 600 Rinehart Road, Lake Mary, Florida 32746, or telephone (407) 333-0600.

THE RUTH ANOINTING by Michelle McClain-Walters
Published by Charisma House
Charisma Media/Charisma House Book Group
600 Rinehart Road
Lake Mary, Florida 32746
www.charismahouse.com

Cover design by Lisa Rae McClure
Design Director: Justin Evans

Visit the author's website at www.michellemcclainwalters.com.

Library of Congress Cataloging-in-Publication Data

Names: McClain-Walters, Michelle, author.
Title: The Ruth anointing / Michelle McClain-Walters.
Description: Lake Mary, Florida : Charisma House, 2018. | Includes
   bibliographical references and index.
Identifiers: LCCN 2018005438 (print) | LCCN 2018019457 (ebook) | ISBN
   9781629994642 (ebook) | ISBN 9781629994635 (trade paper : alk. paper)
Subjects: LCSH: Bible. Ruth--Criticism, interpretation, etc.
Classification: LCC BS1315.52 (ebook) | LCC BS1315.52 .M33 2018 (print) | DDC
   222/.3506--dc23
LC record available at https://lccn.loc.gov/2018005438

19 20 21 22 23 — 7 6 5 4 3
Printed in the United States of America

CONTENTS

YOUR DESTINY IS CALLING

I HAVE ALWAYS had a fascination with Ruth, especially in my days as a single woman. Since the Lord has sent me my Boaz—my wonderful husband, Floyd—my fascination with Ruth burns beyond the revelations believers usually glean from her story. Yes, Ruth's story gives us hope that there is restoration after great loss, a broken heart can be mended, and lost love can be found again. But there is so much more beneath the surface of Ruth's story.

When we dive in deeper, we discover that though Boaz and Ruth found each other as husband and wife, the story of Ruth is not only a romance story. The story of Ruth is also about how broken dreams can become the greatest source of hope. Out of the ashes of disaster, God enabled Ruth to rescue and restore honor to her mother-in-law and create a life and legacy that we are still learning from today. Ruth is an example of dedication and sacrifice. Her life demonstrated how faithfulness and loyalty moved the hand of God to not only touch her life but also enable her to become the hand of God in the lives of others.

Ruth was a pioneer. Moving with Naomi from Moab to Bethlehem, she ventured past cultural limitations and boundaries to discover a life of fulfillment. Understand that this was not a move Ruth had to make. She had family and kinsmen in Moab. She had her gods, religion, and culture that she had grown accustomed to. She did not have to go, but something compelled her to take the risk, step out into the unknown, and travel to a land where she had never been before. She knew she had a destiny to chase, and it would not be fulfilled if she stayed where she was.

Real growth stops when you lose the tension between where you are and where you want to be. Ruth's story challenges us to lean into the tension. Ruth, having lost so much with the death of her husband, did not settle for heartache and pain. She chose to do something different and encountered destiny! One commentary says that "Ruth is an example of the grace of God, inclining the soul to choose the better part."[1] Ruth chose a better life by leaving her old life behind and staying with Naomi. Ruth was willing to risk it all and be stretched to fulfill her destiny! Are you willing to be stretched? Can you be trusted to choose the better part?

Let me say this, beloved: if you are settling for the status quo, you are already disqualified. Stretching involves change. Stretching sets you apart from others. Stretching gives you a shot at significance. Let God stretch you. Like a rubber band, God will stretch you to give you the capacity for more. God is the only One who can stretch you and not break you!

WHAT IS THE RUTH ANOINTING?

In this season God is releasing a pioneering anointing among women that will empower us to break through lives of mediocrity. A *pioneer* can be defined as "a person who is among the first to explore or settle a new country or area...a person who is among the first to research and develop a new area of knowledge, or activity."[2] *Pioneer* also means "develop, introduce, evolve, start, begin, launch, instigate, initiate, put in place…spearhead, institute, establish, found…be the father of, be the mother of, originate, set in motion, create."[3]

Ruth was not afraid to step outside her culture to embrace new possibilities. She left her homeland and all her comfort to pioneer a new life that yielded an unexpected return. As women with the Ruth anointing, we will also be compelled, with a pioneer's anointing upon our lives, to leave our comfort zones and align with God's purposes for our lives. In doing this, things that seemed impossible will become possible. Marked by resolute decisiveness, the Ruth anointing will cause us to make destiny-altering decisions that will catapult us into some of the greatest breakthroughs and discoveries.

We will be challenged to survey and conquer new territories, to do new things, and to develop new and strategic relationships. In this season we cannot be like our old selves; we cannot settle for less. We must go forth with the awareness that we were born for a distinct purpose even if we have not yet figured it out. This is the core of the Ruth anointing— a courageous, bold, faith-filled, and resolute pioneering spirit.

Women with the Ruth anointing will have an uncanny awareness of God's hand and wisdom in the everyday events of our lives. Our only certainty about the future is that God knows it! We must seize every opportunity without fear. The confidence we have lies in knowing who orchestrates our future and that He has our best interests in mind. We must trust in the Lord with all our hearts, leaning not on our own understanding (Prov. 3:5). In times of uncertainty and change God is calling forth women who are committed to Christ, who will flow in the power of the Holy Spirit, and who will face the future with innovation and confidence in the Father's love and care.

Seven Traits That Activate and Cultivate the Ruth Anointing

I truly believe God is going to quicken the process through which women will be introduced to their destinies. As women with the Ruth anointing, we will be able to build and maintain a supernatural level of excellence and purpose because of seven traits.

1. Devotion to God

To know the right time to move out from complacency into a season of great harvest and influence, we need to develop a heart that hears God. Ruth's devotion to God flowed so effortlessly, so resolutely through her life that it enabled her to tune in to the voice and commands of God, to trust Him enough to go when He said go. What is interesting here is that mostly all she knew about the God of Abraham, Isaac, and Jacob came through Naomi's example. Ruth took this example and adapted it to her own life, devoting herself to the ways of God. *Devotion* takes on two meanings here. On one hand, it means "an act of prayer or private worship."[4] The Bible doesn't tell us what Ruth's personal time with God looked like, yet we can see that her actions were those of one well acquainted with the character of God. She was willing to leave everything behind for the God she had come to know. This shows a deep level of faith, and faith comes by hearing the Word of God and experiencing His faithfulness.

Devotion also means "the act of dedicating something to a cause, enterprise, or activity…the fact or state of being ardently dedicated and loyal."[5] Ruth's declaration—"where you go, I will go, and where you lodge, I will lodge. Your people will be my people, and your God, my God. Where you die, I will die, and there I will be buried" (Ruth 1:16–17)—is a demonstration of her devotion, dedication, loyalty, and commitment to her mother-in-law, Naomi, and to God. There was nothing tying her to Naomi anymore after Ruth's husband—Naomi's son—had died. There was no further obligation Ruth had to fulfill, but she stayed with Naomi anyway.

This level of commitment is required of modern-day Ruths. To step out into the unknown, we must be devoted to God and to the people He assigns us to. We must be ready and willing to do whatever we must to stay in His presence so that we can hear and obey Him.

2. Dependency on the direct and deliberate guidance of the Holy Spirit

Modern-day Ruths must develop an intimate relationship with the Holy Spirit. The working of the Holy Spirit was somewhat limited in Ruth's time, but that is not so in our time because of the coming of the Holy Spirit in Acts 2 on the Day of Pentecost. As Ruth received divinely inspired guidance from Naomi, we will receive direct guidance from the Holy Spirit Himself. And we must count on His leading with each step we take. When Jesus spoke of leaving, He said, "And I will ask the Father, and He will give you another Helper (Comforter, Advocate, Intercessor—Counselor, Strengthener, Standby), to be with you forever—the Spirit of Truth, whom the world cannot receive [and take to its heart] because it does not see Him or know Him, but you know Him because He (the Holy Spirit) remains with you continually and will be in you" (John 14:16–17). Beloved, with the Holy Spirit dwelling in you, you will not be left an orphan, a widow, or like any of the forgotten ones. You are remembered, and your days are written in His book. He will be faithful to see you through to your destiny. Depend on His guidance.

3. Honor and virtue

Ruth was a woman of honor and virtue, and she honored others around her. As we will soon discuss, Boaz called Ruth "a virtuous woman" (Ruth 3:11, KJV). As a matter of fact, he said that all the people in town knew Ruth was a virtuous woman. The word *virtue* carries with it a sense of honor and goodness. Looking deeper into the Hebrew translation of the word *virtuous* in this scripture, it carries connotations of strength, efficiency, substance, worth, power, and might.[6] Our modern-day definition of the word *virtuous* is "morally excellent, righteous."[7] It means "decent, ethical, honest, honorable, just, moral, nice, right, righteous, right-minded, straight, true, upright, good."[8]

These traits were evident in Ruth's life. Everyone noticed how she honored Naomi, Boaz, and the workers in the field where she worked. Ruth demonstrated her honor for people by being a resourceful partner first to Naomi and then to Boaz, by taking initiative when there were needs to be met, and by valuing and caring for those around her. She used what she had to make things better. Ruth was fast-tracked to her destiny because of these traits. The same will happen with modern-day Ruths who innately honor the generation that came before them as well as their peers in ministry and in the workplace. They will understand the reciprocal nature of honor, blessing, and favor.

4. Covenantal friendship with other women and strategic alliances with men

Covenantal relationships are key to operating in the Ruth anointing. Too often we use divine connections for our own purposes, not realizing the value of these people in our lives. There is an epidemic of individualism in our culture today that causes us to be so self-centered that we no longer seek to maintain fruitful, long-term relationships with others. But in this season those who receive favor and prosper will be those Ruths who remain loyal and committed to the people God has placed in their lives. They will seek to cultivate deep and abiding connections with men and women of God for the purposes of the kingdom.

5. Courage to leave the old for the new

As we study the life of Ruth, we will discover that she was a barrier breaker. She shattered the status quo and had no hesitation about adopting new customs, behaviors, and practices to be all God commanded her to be. We really need to see this: Ruth left her whole culture behind to embrace the culture of the people of God. She left her religious customs, family, and homeland—all that was familiar—and started again in a new region with a new group of people, and she excelled. Modern-day Ruths will carry within them a spirit that will allow them to move effortlessly among new cultures and nations of the world, bringing the hope and light of God wherever they go. Modern-day Ruths will thrive and excel in new areas and territories. What may seem mysterious and out of reach for others will be accessible and relatable to Ruths. They will possess a necessary sensitivity to cultures and people groups that mirrors the ministry of Jesus, one that is attractive and welcoming to all the people of the world. Diverse nations of the world will be captivated by women who carry the Ruth anointing, wanting to know the God they serve.

6. Humility, submission, and obedience

There is no amount of worshipping, crying at the altar, or any other sacrifice of time, talent, or treasure that can take the place of humility, which gives way to submission to the authority of God and obedience. There is something interesting about Ruth that we will soon uncover that caused her to move into her new life with a level of humility, submission, and obedience so that the Lord could not help but honor His word and grant her uncommon favor in a strange land. When Naomi gave her guidance on what to do next in securing their livelihood, Ruth simply responded, "I will do everything that you say" (Ruth 3:5). This is what God requires of modern-day Ruths. This was not a forced or unnatural response from Ruth. This was the core of who she was—decisive, humble, action-oriented, and focused—and this is one of the keys to seeing Ruth's anointing activated in your life. The Bible says:

> Sacrifice and meal offering You do not desire, nor do You delight in them; You have opened my ears and given me the capacity to hear [and obey Your word]; burnt offerings and sin offerings You do not require. Then I said, "Behold, I come [to the throne]; in the scroll of the book it is written of me. I delight to do Your will, O my God; Your law is within my heart."
>
> —PSALM 40:6–8

> He gives His grace [His undeserved favor] to the humble [those who give up self-importance].
>
> —PROVERBS 3:34

> God is opposed to the proud and haughty, but [continually] gives [the gift of] grace to the humble....So submit to [the authority of] God....Come close to God [with a

contrite heart] and He will come close to you. Wash your hands, you sinners; and purify your [unfaithful] hearts, you double-minded [people]....Humble yourselves [with an attitude of repentance and insignificance] in the presence of the Lord, and He will exalt you [He will lift you up, He will give you purpose].

—JAMES 4:6–10

We see here that Ruth's capacity to be humble, submitted, and obedient invited grace, favor, intimacy with God, and exaltation or promotion to reign in her life. Look for the same to happen in your life as you walk in the Ruth anointing.

7. Stop declaring and get to doing

Many of us have grown accustomed to the idea of name it and claim it, or using the creative power of the tongue to speak things into existence, to speak those things that are not as though they were. I do not question the importance of this, but in terms of forging new territory and stepping out of one's comfort zone, we need to recognize that Ruth did not do a whole lot of talking. Ruth chose her words carefully and released them at strategic moments to set in motion what she was going to do. Later we are going to examine Ruth's "I will" statements and see that her words directly coincided with her actions. She did not state her hopes, wishes, and dreams with the caveat that they one day may or may not happen. Ruth spoke knowing the true power of her words, and she used them to align her will with God's. To activate this same anointing in your life, get ready to do a lot more walking and a lot less talking. The Bible says, "Be ye doers of the word" (James 1:22, KJV).

Four Hindrances That
Hijack the Ruth Anointing

As we come to understand Ruth's pioneering, forward-moving spirit, we are able to identify the hindrances to this anointing. There won't be anything that gets in the way of progress, of moving forward, of breaking through, and of going to a higher level in God and in life. The Scriptures show us that Ruth was unstoppable. She was not going to be turned around by anything. But as we look deep into her story, we see circumstances she faced that could have caused her to give up, turn back, and go home. These are the things that modern-day Ruths must guard against.

It is important for us to know what we are made of, especially in the face of crisis. It's nothing to stand in faith when things are going well. The true measure of the Ruth anointing is shown when life is hard. The first step in overcoming is identifying the enemy. The following is a list of hindrances the enemy will try to throw in your way as you move to the next season.

Idleness

Women with the Ruth anointing are diligent. They do not let themselves become slothful. They know that the hand of the diligent rules (Prov. 12:24). Ruth's virtue would not allow her to eat the bread of idleness (Prov. 31:27). Idleness leads to slothfulness, which is an enemy of diligence.

Cultural biases

We see in the story of Ruth several factors that normally limit an individual's progress in a society. Those factors are racism, sexism, and classism. Ruth was a poor, widowed Moabite woman. In leaving Moab and coming into new culture, she was at the bottom rung of the socioeconomic ladder and could have allowed the social customs of her day dictate how far she could go. But she didn't. She saw these factors as speed bumps on her way to being all God wanted her to be. Ruth blasted through these barriers and became a leading woman in her newly adopted culture, a wife and mother, an owner of the field she once gleaned, and one of the few women named in the lineage of Christ.

Selfishness

Ruth could have had a pity party over the state of her life at the time Naomi decided to leave. She had essentially lost everything, including the hope of being part of an upstanding Jewish family. She could have turned inward and seen all that she was not—a wife, a mother, a member of a prominent family, and on and on. But she didn't. Instead of dwelling on her own losses, Ruth chose to give up everything to see about her mother-in-law's welfare, and in turn she received all that she had lost and more. Modern-day Ruths must be careful not to fall into the trap of self-pity or selfishness. The more that we come to accept God's plan for our lives in blessing others, the more we will come to realize the dreams and desires that He has placed in our hearts. Selfishness will keep us from operating in the full wisdom and favor of God. Selfishness will cause us to focus on our own fears and limitations, and we will forfeit the supernatural power that comes from walking boldly in the unselfish love of God.

Fear of the future

Ruth did not have a fear of the future because she knew who held it. She did not doubt that God was leading her into a good land. Fear of the future will stop modern-day Ruths every time. We will not be able to move forward into new territory if we are overcome with fear. We must be resolute in the knowledge of God's faithfulness to us. We must be confident, knowing that He has a future and a hope for us. This confidence will lead us to take on any challenge and break through every barrier.

WELCOME TO THE PROCESS

The Ruth anointing challenges us to be awakened to what God is doing and to be ready to do as He commands at a moment's notice. Sometimes you can be in the midst of doing a lot of things but not really have revelation of your unique part in God's plan. What I endeavor to do in this book is to give you the tools that will help you find your place and play your part so that when the next opportunity comes, you know where to start. This journey to be the women God created us to be is about taking one step at a time. Some of us get overwhelmed with all the possible things we can do. Others become paralyzed thinking of all the things we cannot do. We look up to other women of faith and think, "Wow, I may never measure up to that." But this is what I learned: the call of God is progressive.

We have our eyes set on this imaginary place called There, but there is really no place called There. Let's get that concept out of our minds. We are on a journey. God is taking us through a process. So I want you to relax. Do not start comparing yourself to where another person is on her journey and wonder why you are not further along. You do not see things the way God sees them. When you do not keep your eyes on Jesus, you will begin to doubt the word He spoke over you. You will start looking around, and fear will begin to set in and you will begin to sink, just like Peter. But I hope you will learn from Ruth and how she fixed her gaze into the heart of God. She never lost sight of God. Fear did not plague her because she stood on an unshakeable faith. She knew she had a destiny bigger than what she was working with at the time.

So for you, beloved, set your eyes on God. Take courage! The journey to your destiny has just taken a whole new turn.

PRAYERS THAT ACTIVATE THE RUTH ANOINTING

The Ruth anointing is about being open to new possibilities. There are many blessings the Lord desires to release in your life, but you must be open to His ways and His thoughts. The story of Ruth begins with famine but ends in harvest. It opens with tragedy but closes in victory. We must understand that God redeems our times and restores the years in our lives that the cankerworm and palmerworm have eaten (Joel 2:25). God's mercy will always triumph over judgment. The Book of Ruth demonstrates how God can take your barrenness and transform it into fruitfulness. This great exchange is central to Ruth's story and to yours. Know that God makes everything beautiful in its time (Eccles. 3:11).

Father, I thank You that my times are in Your hands. You make all things new. I thank You, Lord, that You take the ashes of my life and make them beautiful. Lord, let this be a season of the great exchange. Let the oil of joy be poured into my life for the spirit of mourning. I will no longer mourn what I have lost. Lord, I ask that You will cause my joy to be full. I decree that the joy of the Lord is my strength. I will not wallow in self-pity. I break off the spirits of heaviness, depression, and oppression. I wrap myself in the garment of praise. Instead of the shame of a widow or barren woman, I will have double honor. Instead of confusion, I will walk in revelation and understanding. I will rejoice in my portion. I will embrace the Ruth anointing, and I will pioneer a new path of glory and double honor. I trust You Lord, for where You lead I will follow. In Jesus's name, amen.

ॐ

Father, I pray that You will open my eyes to the new things You are doing in my life. I declare that I will embrace new possibilities. Your plan for me is good and not evil. Your plan is to give me a hope and future. Lord, I believe You speak from my future and that everything in my life is already finished in You. I will arise in faith and depend on You to show me the path of life. What is my path? Lord, I ask that You reveal it to me by Your Spirit.

Father, bring divine connections into my life. Connect me with mentors and coaches who will help me fulfill my destiny. Lord, I ask that You deliver me from dream thieves. Holy Spirit, awaken the dream of the Lord in my life. Make me a blessing to my generation. Let me be favor to someone else.

Where Your Spirit leads me, I will follow. I humble myself under Your mighty hand. I trust that in due season You will exalt me. Lord, You said in Your Word that obedience is better than sacrifice. I will obey Your leadings. I will walk in Your ways. I will trust You with my whole heart, leaning not on my own understanding. Amen.

Chapter 1

I AM RUTH; HEAR ME ROAR

A lion has roared! Who will not fear? The Lord God has
spoken! Who can but prophesy?

—Amos 3:8, nkjv

I BELIEVE WITH every fiber of my being that God has ordered
and predetermined our paths according to His lovingkindness.
The Bible tells us in Psalm 16:11 that God will show us the path
of life. Destiny is a point in our life journey where the reason
we were born finally takes shape. Our eyes are opened to our
potential, and our ears are tuned in to the whisper of our purpose. When destiny settles on us, we are catapulted into our
purpose and nothing can stop us.

Destiny thrives when our wills align with what God has
already established and ordained. Ruth demonstrated this
powerful shift when she stated that she would not return to
her people, but she would travel on with Naomi to another
culture and people, no matter the outcome. She had a sense
that was the exact moment God was calling her to come out
from among her people. She knew that God was calling her
higher, and she answered with a steady, "I will go" (Ruth 1:16).

The resolute nature of Ruth's response silenced any kind
of double-mindedness or instability that the enemy may have
tried to leverage against her during a time of great grief and
loss. When we answer the invitation to partner with God for

our destiny, there should be no waffling or indecisiveness. We can take on the mind of Christ and move forward in mental strength, choosing not just the best way forward but God's way forward. I like what Matthew Henry's commentary says about this: "Those that go in religious ways without a steadfast mind, stand like a door half open, which invites a thief; but resolution shuts and bolts the door, resists the devil and forces him to flee."[1] The decisive nature of the Ruth anointing is like spiritual warfare! As it says in God's Word, "'How long will you hesitate between two opinions? If the LORD is God, follow Him; but if Baal, follow him'" (1 Kings 18:21).

In her few words Ruth respectfully ended the discussion with Naomi—"'Do not urge me to leave you or to turn back from following you; for where you go, I will go…' When Naomi saw that Ruth was determined to go with her, she said nothing more" (Ruth 1:16, 18)—and demonstrated a strong ability to refocus, make the right decisions, and get back in the game of life after the death of her husband and to persevere past the voice of hopelessness in her mother-in-law. Ruth had a supernatural press within her spirit. She had an inner strength, an inner force pulling her toward something greater than her present reality.

This quiet strength is pivotal for women operating within the Ruth anointing. We may not be sure of the exact route God is directing us to take, but our confidence in Him as the leading, guiding force means we will not entertain conversation that is contrary to what God has commanded. This takes a level of inner strength that comes from the indwelling Spirit of God.

If we are going to fulfill our destinies, we must strengthen our inner man in Him. We must rely on the Holy Spirit to defeat any opposition, whether external, such as limiting beliefs put on us by friends and family, or internal, such as our own fears, insecurities, and inferiorities. We must build our-selves up on the foundation of our most holy faith (Jude 20). We cannot allow the enemy to defeat our inner sense of des-tiny. We must conquer and press into our destinies!

God speaks from your future. God is the Alpha and the Omega at the same time. Totality rests in Him. God created every living being with a purpose, and He will release every resource and tool we need to obtain a life of fruitfulness and joy. The mandate for mankind is to be fruitful and multiply, to fill the earth and subdue it, and to have dominion (Gen. 1:28). Where there has been a lack of fruitfulness and even famine, there is a grace in the Ruth anointing to break the power of poverty and lack and live a life of fruitfulness and fulfillment. If you make a commitment to the Lord and His destiny placed upon your life, He will release the resources of heaven to ensure you are redeemed from a life of poverty and pain. Your decisions are the trigger mechanisms to living a life filled with pleasure and purpose. As Psalm 16:11 says, "You will show me the path of life; in Your presence is fullness of joy; in Your right hand there are pleasures forevermore."

These are the days in which the Lord is reshaping and reset-ting destiny. Your mistakes do not define you. There is pur-pose in your life that must be fulfilled. Destiny is God's inner GPS, which leads, guides, pushes, and sometimes reroutes you toward His ordained purpose. The word *destiny* refers to "a predetermined course of events often held to be an irresist-ible power or agency."[2] God has predetermined a sequence of events for us, and our thoughts and ideas, the intents of our hearts, our words, and the relationships we have with others help us live in alignment with the heart of God. Our destinies are determined by how we choose to respond to what the Lord has predetermined. God has placed within each of us a desire for greatness. There is an inner yearning, an irresistible power that comes from God, propelling us toward our future. Even when we have experienced some accomplishments or misfortunes, there is an inner unction that keeps us moving until we reach our God-ordained destiny.

LIONESS ARISING

God has given me a revelation regarding women and the mantle we must pick up as we embrace our destiny in this season—it is the revelation of the lioness. It is easy to spot Ruth's lionlike qualities as we examine her quiet strength and resolve. We do not know how Ruth arrived at the place we find her, carrying an unwavering strength and decisiveness. But if we put ourselves in her shoes, we can imagine that she did not arrive at the place we find her overnight. Even with me, I did not step into being a lioness overnight. I was a cub first. Older women and men took me under their wings and cultivated the anointing and integrity I walk in now. Hunting together, pursuing the mission of the kingdom of God together, increases success.

When I speak to live audiences one of my mainstays is a video of lionesses out on the hunt together. Lionesses are resolute and targeted in their movement as they protect their children and as they hunt. These majestic creatures operate at the peak of their destiny—fierce, poised, and strategically positioned—as they encounter enemies, threats, and opposition, as well as when they are hunting to provide food for their young and the whole pride. When I show the video to an audience, usually filled with women, I encourage them not to get squeamish over the lionesses as they hunt and kill but to see them in the spirit of the kind of anointing we need as women in this hour. There are legacies and generations at stake, and we must be strong, levelheaded, and unified to be victorious.

Lionesses hunt together, and they hunt for the whole pride. Consider this in the life of Ruth. Ruth made a covenantal pledge to come into agreement with Naomi and her life in Bethlehem. Ruth worked in the fields to provide for both of them, and Naomi used her wisdom and influence to help establish a secure lifestyle for Ruth. In turn, all of these actions led to establishing the royal line of David, which led to the birth of Christ. The unity and synchronization expressed in the actions of Ruth and Naomi resulted in provision and security that benefitted the whole line of Christ! Our united front as women can benefit whole communities, cities, and nations for generations to come. And please know that it is not the lions in the pride who accomplish this work—it is the lionesses.

The Lord wants us to understand our position as women. As the lionesses embark on a hunt, there is a fierce and bold strategy, which can only be successful when employed with an unprecedented amount of unity and collaboration. Each lioness has a position, a specialized role, whether it is the alpha lioness (the best hunter) who leads or the other lionesses who encircle the prey from various positions. The lionesses coordinate their movements to surround and ambush their prey. There is always a lioness positioned to block the exit from the area, and if the prey tries to get away, that lioness will be the one to say, "You're not going anywhere. You are surrounded." When the lionesses are all fulfilling their specialized roles, there is the greatest chance of success.[3]

The making of a lioness

God is leading women to take on a whole new level of operation as we push back against the powers of darkness. We have to get an inner fierceness, which is passed down from one generation of spiritual lionesses to another. From Scripture we cannot tell what Ruth's upbringing was like or who may have trained her. We can assume whatever she learned about God and godly conduct, she learned from Naomi. Scholars have concluded that Naomi won Ruth's heart to the God of Israel through her love and kindness:

> By this we see both that Naomi, as became an Israelite, had been very kind and obliging to them and had won their love, in which she is an example to all mothers-in-law, and that Orpah and Ruth had a just sense of her kindness, for they were willing to return it thus far. It was a sign they had dwelt together in unity, though those were dead by whom the relation between them came. Though they retained an affection for the gods of Moab [Ruth 1:15], and Naomi was still faithful to the God of Israel, yet that was no hindrance to either side from love and kindness, and all the good offices that the relation required.[4]

That Orpah and Ruth were willing to travel so far with Naomi on her return to her homeland shows the level of love and unity they had even after their husbands had died. It is interesting to note that Naomi did not try to convert either Ruth or Orpah to the faith of her Jewish ancestors. She let her loving and faithful example take the lead.

Naomi's love and kindness caused Ruth to reject her gods and convert to the God of Israel: "'Entreat me not to leave you, or to turn back from following after you; for wherever you go, I will go; and wherever you lodge, I will lodge; your people shall be my people, and your God, my God. Where you die, I will die, and there will I be buried" (Ruth 1:16–17, NKJV). No more coercion or convincing was done on Naomi's part. Her life led. This seems to be what we sometimes preach from the pulpits of our churches but rarely what we exhibit in our everyday lives.

Naomi, going about her customary practices as a woman of Israel, garnered the loyalty of and a covenantal pledge from a woman with a completely different background. Because of Naomi's strong and leading example, Ruth transferred from one pride to another and became a force to be reckoned with.

It is rare that widowed daughters-in-law remain with the mother-in-law. As Matthew Henry noted, "They not only lifted up their voice and wept, as loth to part, but they professed a resolution to adhere to her [Ruth 1:10]: 'Surely we will return with thee unto thy people, and take our lot with thee.' It is a rare instance of affection to a mother-in-law and an evidence that they had, for her sake, conceived a good opinion of the people of Israel."[5] It can also be surmised that Ruth developed a good opinion of the God of Israel through her interaction with her mother-in-law. From there the training ground was set, and Naomi and Ruth walked together as through the winter season, and upon entering the harvest, they formed an alliance and strategy as alpha lioness and wing that brought provision to their generations and dealt a death blow to the enemy who tried to wipe them out in Moab.

A lioness rightly positioned

God showed me that even the lion, the king of the jungle, had to be taught by a lioness. Yet the lioness still knows her position as demonstrated by the fact that the first one to eat is the king. This is a powerful revelation, one that speaks to the humble collaboration of not only women with women but also women with men. If they can have such order and structure in the animal kingdom, and we are greater than they are, we know we have some growing to do. We need to understand our order. God has given me a passion to see men and women work together by collaboration. It was the devil who, in the Garden of Eden, brought enmity between us. I believe God is restoring unity and collaboration. In several of the books in this series I included chapters regarding male and female collaboration. As women, we can have male mentors get us to that next place. But if we fall into that rejection trap and start saying and believing things such as, "They are going to do things to me because I am a woman," then we can miss our destiny.

Ruth entered the Promised Land as a poor immigrant. Her accent, clothes, and mannerisms caused her to stand out, yet she humbly made her way around the city, looking for ways to provide for Naomi and herself. She did not go searching with a sense of self-pity or entitlement. She went ready to work hard. Because of this she caught the eye of an older man in the community, Boaz, who took it upon himself to look out for her and guide her in the way that would be most profitable for her and her mother-in-law. The favor he showed her got her to her next place. In the end the two formed a partnership through the covenant of marriage that raised Ruth's profile as a mother in Israel. All this was because Ruth stayed in position. She knew that the Lord would make a way for her; she only needed to keep still.

Women are very strong and capable, and we are gifted with intuition and sometimes being able to see things before they happen. But even with this we must hold the position the Lord has placed us in. There is nothing worse than getting ahead of God and missing out on the next right step to our destinies. Like Ruth, we must be willing to move when God says move and stay when He says stay.

AWAKENED AND HEALED

In order to be in line with the Spirit of God like Ruth, we need healing and deliverance. Sin and bondage affect our ability to hear God. Common bondages women deal with are fear, anger, and bitterness, which in Ruth's case could have come from her grief. But Ruth did not carry her grief like a victim. Something must have settled in her mind and spirit the moment she made the declaration of loyalty to Naomi.

For women operating with a Ruth anointing, our deliverance will come quickly. We will be the ones to let it go. We will be the ones to allow God to make our paths straight. Yet in the transition we need to be aware of the snares. We must be delivered from fear, anger, and bitterness. We do not see any of these in operation in Ruth's responses and reactions. But Naomi was a different story. She wore grief and bitterness on her sleeve. Therefore, we must be awakened to which spirit we manifest as we journey toward our destinies.

If you do not investigate your heart and walk through whatever healing and deliverance you need, you will find yourself ministering or leading with a voice of anger and bitterness. You will find yourself doing more harm than good. I believe that as we are awakened, we will become an army of women who understand the compassion of God. We are going to be motivated by love. We are going to be empowered by the Holy Ghost, and we are going to be filled with compassion. We are going to move forth with wisdom. It is a new day and a new season in which we will not be governed by our fleshly emotions.

Though Naomi experienced great losses and was somewhat in her flesh, it was her compassion, kindness, and love that initially won Orpah and Ruth to her God. This is the same kind of compassion that will be poured out into the hearts of women with the Ruth anointing. As we move along in the story, you will see how Ruth's demonstration of love and care toward her mother-in-law was in direct relationship to the love that Naomi had shown her all those years in Moab.

One thing that can happen if we are operating out of brokenness is that we seek success in the wrong area. Many of us can testify to a time when we were not sure of our identity and all we desired was to find significance in something—more labels, more degrees, more trips to the nations. Some of us are in that place now.

I remember a time when I had my identity in how many nations I traveled to. Other ministers and I would compare how many stamps we had in our passports. "I have ten," one of us would say. "Well, I have fifteen," another would answer back. "I have twenty-five." Those were nothing but fig leaves that we put on to make us feel like somebody.

Generally speaking, there is nothing wrong with those things, but what you need is to be secure if all those things were taken away from you. You want to be able to still stand without them, saying, "I live my life before the King. I obey Him. I can sit in the front, or I can sit in the back. This stuff does not define me. If I have to walk away from it, I will."

If God says, "Let it go—I have something new for you," or if He calls you to walk out on the water, and your identity is tied to that stuff, how will you be able to step out? Ruth left everything behind! We need to become women who say, "I am determined to live nothing but Jesus Christ and Him crucified. I am not for sale. My gift is not for sale." Every commitment, every label, and every degree or accomplishment is not part of your God-ordained assignment, your call, or your process. If you are caught up in these things, you are caught up in trying to get somebody to recognize you. But hear me, beloved: You are already beautiful. You are already bought. You are already experienced. You need to encounter the God of your call. He will help you to know what to invest in and what to move on from.

ENCOUNTERING THE GOD OF YOUR CALL

Encountering the God of your call is all about seeing yourself and your ministry from God's perspective. When you see yourself in the light of God's glory, it brings the fear of the Lord and a level of resolve and determination to complete your assignment in the earth. When you get a real awakening in your life, you begin to evaluate everything you do. Everything is on the chopping block. You will catch yourself uttering the lines of that game show *Weakest Link*: "You are the weakest link. Good-bye." When I crossed the threshold of fifty years old, something changed. I found myself thinking, "No, I am not doing that." Listen, beloved, Chaka Khan lied to us. We are not every woman. It is not all in us. No. We are only who God designed us to be. The urgency for living up to that comes when we can say, "I have encountered the God of my call."

There seems to be a split-second encounter with Jehovah that Ruth had just before she made her declaration to Naomi. In that moment she knew what she had to do to grab on to her destiny. God called her and confirmed her in that moment. She did not even say good-bye. Are you ready for this?

Whether you are a doctor, lawyer, or day care provider, you will do all you do because it falls in line with who God created you to be. You will move with a resolve that says, "If it's up, I'm there. If it's down, I'm there. If I have to do it alone, I will do it alone. I am doing this because I have encountered the God of my call." We must look to encounter the God of our call as Isaiah did. We all need an Isaiah 6 experience. Isaiah said, "I saw the Lord sitting on a throne, high and lifted up" (v. 1, NKJV). And when he saw God, he saw himself.

In the light of God's glory we come to see ourselves so clearly that we will be moved to change. Against God's glory, we will begin to see what isn't right in our lives, what doesn't fit in with the plans He has for us. This is not just about sin and repentance; this is also very much about purpose and not just the good things we do but the God things. Encountering God in the close way Isaiah did and then being cleansed with the coal from the altar is a life-altering, paradigm-shifting experience. It changes everything. What we thought was right is challenged. I can hear God saying, "Come up a little higher, my daughter." We encounter the ways and thoughts of God at this level. We come to understand why the word of the Lord through Isaiah is, "My thoughts are not your thoughts, nor are your ways My ways" (Isa. 55:8). As we encounter God's glory, we begin to truly see ourselves—who we are and who we are not. We begin to see the gulf between where we are and where God wants us to be. A whole new and holy self-examination process happens in this place. Light begins to separate from darkness, the soul from the spirit. Our purpose and destiny become clearer. They are fortified in the presence of almighty God.

Then the God of our call helps us to see the people He is calling us to. Remember, the pull of destiny is not only about you. In the encounter with his Creator, Isaiah is humbled and says, "Woe is me, for I am undone! Because I am a man of unclean lips" (Isa. 6:5, NKJV). His humility turns into an awareness that the people he is called to are in the same boat: "And I dwell in the midst of a people of unclean lips" (Isa. 6:5, NKJV). This awareness of the condition of the people around him turn into an urgency and compassion to serve and minister to them. He says, "Here am I! Send me!" (Isa. 6:8, NKJV). This is what the Lord was calling Him to. This is what He was purifying for and equipping Him to do. As he encountered the presence of God, Isaiah was made aware of what he was designed to do.

Seeing our call in the light of God's glory changes everything. It makes us come to life, come to purpose, and come to destiny, letting go of everything else. Encountering the God of our call brings focus to our lives and all we do. Our faces become like flint (Isa. 50:7). We know what we need to do. No fear, no mountains, no giants—nothing else matters. Every other thing that comes against our assignment, whether it is the fiery darts of the enemy or past sin, will not dictate our future. Ruth left everything, and the only thing she had was her future. Encountering the God of your call puts a "go" in your spirit and propels you forward. Upon encountering God, you will be compelled to say, "Send me. I'll go."

Women, I want you to understand that when you are faced with the opportunity to do this fearless thing, you will gain the confidence you need by making time to meet with the King. You will find strength to stretch and take on challenging new things that catapult you into your next place when you sit in the presence of God. The call of the prophet Isaiah began with his vision of the Lord, seated high and lifted up. This viewpoint also caused him to see a reflection of himself and his need for the presence of God to cleanse him and accompany him into the next phase of his assignment. Being in the presence of God caused him to see that the people he had been hanging around were unclean too. As I have already said (and cannot really say enough), it is important to pray for divine connections.

Not only should we be desperate to encounter the God of our call, but we should also want to be around people who will encourage and lift us up in our call. Do not let someone else direct you away from your call. Do not be moved by anyone else's words and manipulation. Be moved by what God says. I believe this was why there was no pushback from Naomi once Ruth made her choice. Naomi knew how her God worked. Naomi did not get in the way of Ruth hearing from the God of her call on her own. Naomi even upped the ante by suggesting that it was a bad idea for Ruth to leave her home. She did this to drive home Ruth's sure conviction so that Ruth could say, "Yes, this is what the God of my call says is right for me: 'Whither thou goest, I will go...' (Ruth 1:16, KJV)." In so many ways, these words make up Ruth's roar—her declaration to follow Naomi and her God to the grave. Can you hear the quiet fierceness behind her words?

Roar, Ruth. Roar!

PRAYERS THAT ACTIVATE THE ROAR

I will not be silent. I will open my mouth and speak the truth of the Lord. I will be a voice for the voiceless.

I decree that every muzzle is removed from my mouth. By the power of Your Spirit let every muzzle of fear be removed from my mouth. I will be the voice of justice.

I am fearless and fierce. I will walk in the fullness of my call. I will chase my dreams. I will seek out opportunity to be light in a dark world.

I decree: Let there be great awakening in my soul. Let the fire of the Holy Ghost consume me. I embrace the boldness of the lioness.

Holy Spirit, awaken my spirit. I decree I am a go-getter. I will not draw back from the challenges of life. I will live my destiny. I decree that I will live a passion-filled life. I will be bold and strong. Lord, strengthen me with might in my inner man. I am strong in the Lord and the power of His might.

Prayer That Invokes the Presence of the God of Your Call

Father, I ask that You give me Your heart for my life. Enlighten the eyes of my understanding. Help me to know why You created me. What did we talk about before I was in my mother's womb? What were You thinking when You knit me in my mother's womb? Fill my heart and my mind with Your thoughts toward me.

Lord, I desire to do everything You purposed me to do. Give me grace to fulfill Your call on my life. Lord, I need a holy visitation. Pour out the Spirit of knowledge upon my life. I want a living understanding of who I am before Your throne. Cause me to see life from Your perspective.

I want to see You high and lifted up. Lord, I want to know You. In Your presence is the fullness of joy. Lord, show me the path of life. Lord, my soul thirsts for You. Come, Holy Spirit, and quench my thirst. I seek Your face. I long to see Your power and Your glory.

God, give me revelation of who You are. Remove scales from eyes. I long to see humanity from Your perspective. Lead me, and guide me. I want to be sent from Your presence. Take the coal from Your heavenly altar and cleanse me from any iniquity and sin that would hinder my call. In Jesus's name, I pray. Amen.

Chapter 2

SEASONS OF DESTINY

Let us not grow weary or become discouraged in doing good, for at the proper time we will reap, if we do not give in.

—GALATIANS 6:9

DESTINY BEGINS WITH a seed, and every one of us has the seed of destiny inside. The Bible says that God has "planted eternity [a sense of divine purpose] in the human heart [a mysterious longing which nothing under the sun can satisfy, except God]" (Eccles. 3:11). This longing is toward a purpose or destiny so big we cannot fathom it. It is beyond our comprehension. But there is a part for us to discover, act on, and reap from.

God is looking for those who will plant and cultivate the seed of destiny He planted within them. He is most interested in promoting men and women who are fruitful—those who will not only talk about it but will also be about it, those who are ready to do something. If you know that the Lord is calling you into your destiny, you cannot afford to remain in the company of people who do nothing. In the same way they place limitations upon themselves, they will attempt to imprison you with their expectations of who you should be—things that they think are dictated by color, gender, social class, or economic status. But do not fall victim to this mentality, becoming hitched to societal balls and chains. The awareness of the purpose and destiny of God provides all the force you need to face opposition. That awareness will ground you when resources do not line up with the vision. It will give you the faith and courage you need to step into the vision. Provision, favor, and finances will come when you start doing it. People will help when you start picking it up.

Ruth did not have anything. All the odds were stacked against her, but something in her did not let her stay in her broken place. I believe she was always a woman who was not afraid to take a risk. She stepped outside the status quo and married a man from a different culture. Ruth had a different spirit—the spirit of Caleb and Joshua, one that saw the future through God's eyes despite the attempts of the enemy to sabotage her destiny. Like the occupying enemies Caleb and Joshua had to run out of the Promised Land, Ruth also had to go to war against giants such as grief, poverty, and social and cultural customs that attempted to steal her next level. And like them, she conquered them all and reached her promised land.

Just because you cannot see your way through does not mean you cannot do it. "I don't have enough" is a spirit, but the spirit you should adopt in this season is the one of more than enough.

Modern-day Ruths may be faced with poverty, unemployment, and loss and grief of various kinds. But hardships force you to make a move or choose to lie there and die. Hardships cause you to make decisions. We will study how every time Ruth was in a tight spot, she made a choice to keep moving, and every time she moved, favor followed. Favor did not come before the decision to move; it came after. Eventually she ended up in her destiny, what I call her "wonderful place."

Let God Bring You
Through the Winter

Many times when we feel the pull of destiny, we also feel the pull of the past. The enemy will use this to create fear, causing us to believe that if we move forward, somehow the things we have done in the past will come back to sabotage our future. We fear that just as we get comfortable in our new lives, God will come back like a reaper to collect for our past failures. But let me encourage you with this: God is good, and His mercy triumphs over judgment. Yes, there is a season in life when we are taking inventory and God is showing us areas in which we need to step up. We are shown the not-so-great parts of ourselves, the parts of ourselves that are not aligned with God and His purpose for our lives, the parts we need to repent of and receive deliverance—and this is good!

In *The Deborah Anointing* I highlighted four spiritual seasons we go through in life: winter, spring, summer, and fall. The season I am referring to here is spiritual winter:

> Spiritual winter can seem like a time of darkness, as if your life is unfruitful, and you may assume your dreams are dying. But during winter there is no fruit bearing. It is a time when God kills everything in your life that will affect the harvest of the next season in your life. Spiritual winter is the most uncomfortable time for many Christians. However, this is a season to redefine and further develop a relationship with the God of your call. This is when God continues to develop your root system in Him. There He will give you directions for planting new crops in spring....Spiritual winter is the time for evaluation, planning, and preparation. It is a time for letting go of anything that will destroy your call. It is also the time to learn the uniqueness of your call.[1]

We know from the story of Ruth that Naomi's husband, Elimelech, led his family out of Bethlehem, which was in the land of Canaan, the land flowing with milk and honey, and went to Moab to escape a famine. By all accounts this was his attempt to provide for his family and shield them from the effects of the famine. But the famine was a pronouncement of God against the people of Israel for not walking according to the covenant God had established with them. (See Leviticus 26:19–20.) If we are wise, we know that we cannot outrun the judgments of God, which are many times the consequences of our own sin. We must remember that God chastens those He loves (Heb. 12:6–7).

We do not benefit when we try to shorten these times of loving chastening. There are things that God does in this season that cannot be done at any other time. Winter builds within us the character to handle the harvest that begins to break forth in the spring season. And though Elimelech moved his family out of the line of fire, they did not escape their winter season. In fact, his actions may have caused it to be more intense. Matthew Henry's commentary says this: "Elimelech's care to provide for his family, was not to be blamed; but his removal into the country of Moab could not be justified. And the removal ended in the wasting of his family."[2] In the first chapter of Ruth we find that Elimelech died in Moab. His sons, Mahlon and Chilion, then married Moabite women, which was not in accordance with the Israelites' covenant with God. They were not to marry women of idolatrous nations. But they did, and the sons died as well.

So we can see that in the end Elimelech's attempt to move his family out of harm's way came up short, and his family was worse off than if they had stayed in Bethlehem. He did not give himself or his family the blessing of strength and fortitude that comes as a result of enduring the winter season. They did not get a chance to see what was fruitful and what was not, what to hold onto and what to let go of. The same is true for us: we do not get to experience the full working of the Lord when we try to dodge the process.

THEN COMES SPRING

I will talk in more detail about Naomi as we get further into her spiritual role in influencing the Ruth anointing, but it is important to recognize here that Naomi was the catalyst for the turnaround in her and Ruth's destinies. Naomi's decision to return to obedience by returning to her homeland righted her husband's wrong of leaving the Promised Land in the first place. By returning to obedience, she was also reinstituting, or reinvoking, the covenant blessing of the Lord on her life and the life of her family, which now included Ruth.

By Naomi's willingness to go back home and face the shame of her desolation and take on the winter season on her husband's behalf, she pushed Ruth into her spring season, allowing her to be rewarded once again with a happy marriage and family, to walk in honor among a foreign people, and to live with the abundance promised to God's chosen. By this she also made a way for Ruth to fulfill the most significant part of her destiny, which was being a mother in the line of Christ. What is even more significant is that Ruth's time of winter was shortened. Upon her declaration in Ruth 1:16–17—"where you go, I will go, and where you lodge, I will lodge. Your people will be my people, and your God, my God. Where you die, I will die, and there I will be buried. May the LORD do the same to me [as He has done to you], and more also, if anything but death separates me from you"—Ruth made a covenant with Naomi and in turn with God. From that moment Ruth made herself available for God to prune and purge all the things that may have stood in the way of her destiny. There was a distance of fifty miles from Moab to Bethlehem, and during the time of that journey Ruth was being prepared for her harvest. As the story goes, she and Naomi "arrived in Bethlehem at the beginning of the barley harvest" (Ruth 1:22). Ruth's winter time was quickened, and she was moved right into a place to reap the spring harvest.

Women who carry the Ruth anointing at this time in history can also expect the Lord to hasten their progress into areas of honor and great influence. But we cannot walk in this level of destiny without first being willing to go through whatever it takes to be a ready vessel for the Lord to fill. Ruth was willing to die and be buried with Naomi. Her loyalty and commitment was unto death. We cannot expect a fruitful harvest if we are not willing to give everything for it. Jesus said, "For whoever wishes to save his life [in this world] will [eventually] lose it [through death], but whoever loses his life [in this world] for My sake will find it [that is, life with Me for all eternity]" (Matt. 16:25). Again, Ruth chose the better thing. Women with the Ruth anointing will have their eyes set on eternity. Their decision-making will be based on what the Lord showed them during the winter season. When spring comes, there will be no hesitation to act on the word of God they already received. Because of this, there will be no delay in the favor and blessing that will pour out onto their lives.

Marked by Redemption

Transitioning us from winter to spring, the Ruth anointing centers around the rush of divine empowerment that God sends directly from His presence to enable us to overcome every obstacle life throws in our paths. Not only will we overcome, but we will also become a source of healing and deliverance for others. Some of us may feel that our time to be an influence has passed because of delays we put in our own way, but I am here to tell you that God is in the business of redeeming abandoned, broken, and forgotten dreams. In this season the Lord is pouring out His mercy and giving many of us a second chance. Your race, gender, or economic status does not matter; the Lord is redefining and, in many cases, defining *destiny*.

Destiny is not decided; it is discovered, and within the Ruth anointing is a special extension of the grace and mercy of God to redeem the time in discovering and acting upon our destinies. The story of Ruth teaches us that the mercy of the Lord is new every morning, it triumphs over judgment, and it endures forever. The Book of Ruth carries within its pages the powerful message of redemption, which is a manifestation of God's mercy to a soul that would choose Him. Ruth is a book about a second chance. It teaches us how we can access the power of God's redeeming love simply by activating our power of choice and devotion. One commentary says that Ruth's resolution to follow Naomi rather than return to her own people was the key to shutting down the work of the enemy in her life. She did not waver. Her decisiveness shut and bolted the door, resisted the devil, and forced him to flee.[3] Can we see this for ourselves? Simply, yet assertively say to the Lord, "Where You lead, I will follow, and where Your presence dwells, I will dwell. The people whom You call by Your name will be my people." (See Ruth 1:16.) This is a powerful and necessary declaration to make to the Lord as we submit to His way of restoring and redeeming us.

As we delve further into the Book of Ruth, her story will begin to satisfy some of the yearning of our souls for deliverance. It will highlight our reasons for the hope we have in

Christ our Redeemer. We will also see the theme of extraordinary service that results in extraordinary blessings. Ruth serves as clear proof that God desires those from all backgrounds to follow Him and that He can work in our lives in tremendous ways to influence the lives of many.

There is a company of women who will have the resolve and resilience to pioneer in new territories. They will not wallow in self-pity or carry a victim mentality. They will not settle for whatever life throws at them. Modern-day Ruths will be empowered by the spirit of the pioneer, leaving old things behind and pressing in to the new.

Your place of deliverance can turn into your place of captivity if you do not stay ready to move when the Spirit says move. Some places were designed for your deliverance, but they were not meant to be your home. Be careful not to let what God used for a season become a place of stagnation. At the core of the Ruth anointing is a readiness to move out of complacency at a moment's notice. Are you ready to move?

PRAYER TO RELEASE THE SPIRIT
OF THE SONS OF ISSACHAR

Lord, Your Word says that the sons of Issachar had understanding of the times and knew what Israel should do. I ask that You release that same grace upon my life. I decree that I am a woman who understands the times of my life. I will move in complete synchronization with Your timing.

Lord, give me the wisdom of the sons of Issachar to understand the times I live in. Lord, I ask that You keep me in perfect time with You. Let me not get ahead of Your process. I ask for grace to endure.

Lord, I also pray that I learn the times and season of my generation. I desire to understand them. I want to understand my culture. Lord, I ask You to give me heavenly insight to effectively engage my culture. In Jesus's name, amen.

Chapter 3

LEAVING THE FAMILIAR

Listen carefully, I am about to do a new thing, now it will spring forth.

—ISAIAH 43:19

WE ALL LOVE to talk about new things—new possibilities, new opportunities, new jobs, new houses, new clothes, and so on. There is just a level of joy associated with new things. However, before we can accept new things into our lives, we must let go of the old things. Whenever God is opening a new chapter in the story of our lives, there is an ending to an old chapter. New is wonderful, but sometimes the circumstances around entering the new can be challenging or even downright painful.

God has determined new things for His daughters, but being in position to receive them will require leaving familiar relationships, methods, and systems to embrace the new things. Transitioning from old to new requires patience, partnership, and perseverance. If we are going to embrace the new, we must understand the process of transition. It will require both a new sense of purpose and boldness to step outside every religious box. It will take going through a process of disconnecting and reconnecting.

Many times when looking for newness, humanity tends to look for it without God. Many want new things on their own terms. Ruth took a risk and left the familiar for her destiny.

Life begins when we leave our comfort zones. Ruth whole-heartedly embraced a new culture, new home, and new religion. The new things that came into Ruth's life did not come to her on her terms. She had to bend her will to the Lord's in order to walk into her next season.

FORGETTING THOSE THINGS WHICH ARE BEHIND

The apostle Paul said, "…forgetting those things which are behind and reaching forward to those things which are ahead, I press toward the goal to the prize of the high calling of God in Christ Jesus" (Phil. 3:13–14, MEV). The hardest part about leaving familiar things is forgetting the old things. Memory is a powerful mechanism. If you hear a sound or smell a fragrance, a memory can be activated. I believe that we can have a soul tie with a city or culture. We love our creature comforts. There is no stylist like my hairstylist. No other grocery store sells just the right cut of meat. Then there are also friends, family, and the community that we would also miss. Familiar environments and the people connected to them can get a hold on us and cause us to stay too long in a season of life when God is ready to move us up and out. We must be deliberate and intentional about letting go of the past to embrace the future.

Another thing to consider is that the fear of the unknown can even cause us to stay in circumstances we hate or are miserable in. This fear is brought on by believing lies about ourselves and others, such as "You aren't worth it," "You're not talented enough," "God is not speaking to you," "You'll never make friends like the ones you have here," "You won't find a place to live and settle into—not like this," or "If you leave, you'll be forgotten." Lies like this can convince us to stay where we are. They can lead us to believe that we are better off settling for known misery than setting out on a journey to the unknown place God is wanting to move us into.

I believe the power of the Ruth anointing lies partly in a refusal to succumb to the draw to stay in a familiar environment. She also refused to become a victim of her circumstances. She had an ability to see opportunity knocking at the door and did not hesitate to answer, which allowed her to walk right into the greatest future she could ever imagine. Women with a Ruth anointing will have inner strength to rise above their pasts, and with tenacity and perseverance they will fulfill their destinies.

KEYS TO SUCCESSFULLY TRANSITIONING FROM OLD TO NEW

Transition requires movement, change, and in some cases relocation. *Transition* can be defined as "the process or a period of changing from one state or condition to another."[1] Other words associated with *transition* are *change, passage, move, transformation, conversion, metamorphosis, alteration,* and *changeover.*[2] Leaving the old for something new carries uncertainty and fear, but the end result is growth and maturity.

God orchestrates and orders our steps through seasons of transition. Although they may seem elusive and sometimes unsure, you can rest knowing that God has established steps for your transition that will work together for your good. The mighty God we serve is both omniscient (all-knowing) and omnipotent (all-powerful). He is not bound by time. God speaks to your present situation from the future, and since you know that He sees your end, you can trust where He is taking you.

Whether for positive reasons or less fortunate reasons, transition is not an easy process. Many of us do not like too much change at one time, and transition challenges our knowledge base and routines. We may think of all the time it took for us to finally understand where we are now, making us hesitant to go through another life transition. But God is with us, and He has made a way for us to have good success. Here are some keys to experiencing a successful transition whether you are leaving a traumatic circumstance, or God is simply saying, "Come up higher."

Live a life dedicated and submitted to God.

Ruth dedicated her life to God, which is the wisest thing a person can do. This puts you in position to hear God's leading and feel His hand on your life. When God speaks to us, many times we are turned inward, thinking about what we want, what we can do, and what we feel comfortable with. This is what a modern Ruth cannot do. It must be "not my will but Your will be done." Sometimes we are in what I call "self-will." As we submit to God, we resist the devil and he will flee (James 4:7). When we submit to God, we cause the enemy to lose his grip on what God has promised us. When we say, "No, I can't do it"—and women are infamous for uttering these words of false humility—we are still looking at self, at what we can or cannot do. Believe it or not, we are manifesting a spirit of pride when we don't say yes to God because we see our inability. We are also manifesting unbelief and doubt in the power of God.

Being dedicated and submitted to God means that we know and trust God's ability to work through us when He calls us to something. We are quick to say, "Yes, God," because we trust and believe that He is with us and will equip us for the task ahead. You've heard the phrase "Shoot first, ask questions later"? Well, I am reclaiming that for the kingdom. Women with the Ruth anointing say yes to God and ask questions later. This is when it really counts. I am not saying that God is not open to questions. But if our questions are formed out of doubt and fear, they are just ways to delay our purpose. Women with the Ruth anointing have met the God of their call. They are faithful, dedicated, committed, and loyal to God and His call on their lives. They believe His promises and obey Him without hesitation. They are single-minded, steadfast, focused, and ready.

Put your trust in the God who owns your future.

Transition requires trusting God and being open to His plans and purposes, not your own. Proverbs 3:5–6 says, "Trust in the LORD with all your heart, and lean not on your own understanding; in all your ways acknowledge Him, and He shall direct your paths" (NKJV). The story of Ruth is about physically, spiritually, emotionally, and culturally transitioning from one place to another. Throughout her journey Ruth kept her eyes on God, trusting that He had a plan for her future.

When we feel anxious or unsure, it is because of our inability to see what God sees. God's Word is a lamp to our feet and a light to our path (Ps. 119:105), but He generally only gives us enough light to see the next step. We may want to be able to see miles down the road, but God wants us to trust Him for every step. We are limited in how far we can see into the future, but God is not. He sees the end from the beginning. And He not only sees the end from the beginning, but He also declares and orchestrates them.

> I am God, and there is none like Me, declaring the end from the beginning, and from ancient times things that are not yet done, saying, "My counsel shall stand, and I will do all My pleasure."
>
> —ISAIAH 46:9–10, NKJV

As Ruth did, we can trust that the future God envisions for us is a good one. In Jeremiah 29:11 He says, "For I know the plans and thoughts that I have for you...plans for peace and well-being and not for disaster, to give you a future and a hope." God brought Ruth out of a place of grief and poverty into a place of hope and abundance. This is His plan for you as well.

Maintain inner strength and courage.

Cultivating inner strength and courage is important for developing the Ruth anointing. They are intangible tools that you should pray for. The Bible says in Ephesians 3:16, "May He grant you out of the riches of His glory, to be strengthened and spiritually energized with power through His Spirit in your inner self, [indwelling your innermost being and personality]." Petition God for the strength and courage to stick with Him through the ups and downs of the transition.

There are four ways that you can be strengthened and energized while you transition:

1. Read and study the Word of God. As you take in God's Word, treasure it in your heart and you will be strengthened in faith, knowing and believing the promises of God. His Word will also keep you secure in Him, reminding you of His ways and His righteousness. Psalm 119:11 says, "Your word I have treasured and stored in my heart, that I may not sin against You."

2. Take every thought captive (2 Cor. 10:5). As we have already identified, women with the Ruth anointing have their minds set on the direction God has told them to go. When you catch and cast out wrong

or negative thinking, you maintain focus on the things of God that can't be shaken.

3. Put on the armor of God (Eph. 6:10–18). As I pointed out in the *The Anna Anointing*, "Paul gives the key to entering into effective warfare prayer: you must be dressed properly. Putting on the whole armor of God requires intentionality. Putting on the armor assures you of victory in the spirit. Just as you have to go to the closet and select clothing to wear for the day, you should put on the armor of God every day. You must not take any short-cuts when putting on the armor. Every piece must be worn to provide protection and strength. There is a synergy of strength and power released to the fully armed soldier. Putting on the armor of God requires making a decision daily to live as a soldier in the army of the Lord."[3]

4. Be on guard, stand firm, be courageous, and be strong. This is a fourfold command from 1 Corinthians 16:13, and it has everything to do with our faith in God. Faith is the great stabilizer of mind and spirit. Faith is the counterbalance to fear. Faith brings peace, and the peace of God guards our hearts and minds in Christ Jesus (Phil. 4:7). The command reflects the verse in Proverbs that says that we need to guard our hearts for out of them flow the issues of life (Prov. 4:23). A strong heart is a courageous heart. Be strong and courageous is also a recurring command in the Bible. God told Joshua to be strong and courageous because He would be with him wherever he would go (Josh.

1:9). Inner strength and courage are about how much we are able to elevate God's strength over ours. And it is not a suggestion, it is a command.

Make a definite cut with the past.

When the Lord is transitioning you to a new place, you must let go of old mind-sets. Transition is the space in between the old place and the new place. The person in transition is not who she used to be, but she is not quite who she is going to be. But in every transition there needs to be a definitive decision made to leave what needs to be left and be ready to move when it is time to move.

Ruth made a clear cut with the past by leaving everything behind. She left her father and mother and clung to her mother-in-law. She left her hometown and relocated to a new city. She recanted her belief in her gods and committed to serve the one true God. She released the season of grieving for her dead husband and welcomed the chance for new love and marriage. These were the actions that followed Ruth's declaration in Ruth 1:16–17. She made a decision and moved forward in it.

Your transition may not be so drastic. You must hear from the Lord. Then once He shows you what He is calling you to do, make the declaration and then move. Let go of what God is commanding you to let go of and embrace what He is leading you to embrace.

Keep moving.

Transition requires movement and momentum. If you stop in the middle of transition, it could mean death—spiritual, emotional, or in Ruth's and Naomi's case, physical. The whole reason they were not staying in Moab, the reason that could not stop midway between Moab and Bethlehem, is because if they stopped, they would have eventually died. They had no money, no food, and no provision to sustain them. Yet Naomi knew that if they kept going, they would be just in time for the harvest season and they would be fed and in the atmosphere of the blessing of God that had recently come back to Israel. They had to keep moving.

For Ruth, it was a bit more. Destiny was pulling her and propelling her forward. God had a plan for her. If she stopped, she would have killed everything tied to her destiny. Ruth was to be a mother in the line of Christ. Her commitment to keep moving and answering the call of her destiny was connected to the salvation of the world.

If you stop before you get to the place God has for you, you can die spiritually where you are. When you stop and settle, your spiritual muscles can atrophy and you become immobilized. This can be one of the consequences for getting out of the flow of God. You must keep moving. As you move when God moves, you stay in line with His timing. Ruth and Naomi made it right on time for the harvest. The conditions were ready; this was the place God was preparing for them—a place that would have everything they needed. If they hesitated or took their time, they would have missed it.

When you are moving by faith, when you have said your initial yes and started moving in the direction God commanded, your hesitation, stalling, or delay will cause you to lose momentum, giving faith a chance to turn to fear. You cannot stop there because you have nothing to go back to and nothing where you are. You must keep moving toward your destiny.

Be ready to learn new modes and methods of operation.

Ruth had to learn a whole new way of life. She had lived as a Moabite her whole life and was now coming into a land where people did everything differently than what she was used to. Ruth succeeded because she was open to new things and willing to learn. She excelled because she listened to her mentor, Naomi, who trained her in the ways of the new culture. The Bible tells us that obedience is better than sacrifice (1 Sam. 15:22). Ruth's willingness and obedience to the counsel of Naomi was crucial to her survival.

Modern-day Ruths must honor the wisdom of the previous generations. When God shifts you to a new place, He also gives you new methods to operate in. You must be flexible and fluid in your new place. Transition results in new roles and new responsibilities, and you must be willing to learn and adapt to a new way of doing things. At times the changes may be minor, but at other times God may call you to make significant changes. Your job is to be willing to change, grow, and learn, regardless of the circumstances.

Seek out and cling to wise counsel.

The Bible says, "Abhor what is evil. Cling to what is good" (Rom. 12:9, NKJV). Being surrounded by wise and godly counsel is good. In fact, unlike a fool who comes up with their own ideas of how to do things, a wise person listens to counsel (Prov. 12:15). So not only is the counsel wise, but we demonstrate wisdom when we seek it out. Skillful and godly wisdom is principal, and we gain wisdom from a multitude of counselors.

We are bombarded with people's opinions about what we should do and how we should carry out what God has called us to. But we should only be holding on to those things that help us accomplish our assignment. One way to do this is to be surrounded by a multitude of wise counselors. In our modern lives this would be your inner circle of friends, family, advisors, and mentors who know the call of God on your life and are committed to see you walk in it.

Ruth listened to Naomi's counsel. Naomi was older, experienced in the ways of God, and a faithful wife and mother. She had lived wisely the path that Ruth was embarking. Job 12:12 says, "With the aged [you say] is wisdom, and with long life is understanding." In Titus 2:3–5 older women are encouraged to teach younger women.

Ruth also listened to Boaz, who gave her direction on how to get what grain she needed to feed Naomi and herself (Ruth 2:8–9). Ruth didn't go about her pursuit of her destiny with the mind-set that she had everything she needed within herself. She was open to the people God placed in her path. She was open to being taught and advised about this new place she had come to.

Her relationships with both Naomi and Boaz are models for mentorship and wise counsel. When looking for someone to advise you on something you are dealing with in life, look for someone who is experienced and successful in what you are trying to obtain. The person should be someone you can look up to and admire. Also, you don't need to look for every aspect of your call to be exemplified in one person. Many times you may get one piece of advice from one person and another piece from someone else. Bringing the counsel together in prayer before God can help you transition successfully. Remember, there is safety in a multitude of counselors (Prov. 11:14).

A Different Spirit

In studying Ruth, I have come to believe that her anointing is not about having the future figured out and being able to rest in knowing she had uncovered and analyzed the full picture of what God was doing. Instead, the Ruth anointing is about being faithful with what God says today, following through on it today, and trusting Him with tomorrow. God has also shown me that this is the spirit that masters the transition from old to new, from comfortable to unfamiliar, and from mediocre to great.

In our culture we are challenged to dream big, set goals, and make plans that scare us so that we can trust God to fulfill them. But I do not see this with Ruth. She was not ambitious in this way. She did not have big plans for the future. She completely, quietly, calmly, and confidently surrendered her life in Moab to go with her mother-in-law—not even her own mother—to a place she did not know, to live with a people she did not know. Who does that? Only a Ruth. The prophetess Deborah did not have this characteristic. She was very goal oriented. She set the bar high and knew God had given her the strength and intellect to get it done. Esther's journey was upended by kidnapping. She ended up in a place not of her choosing. Anna's movement was mostly in the spirit through prayer and intercession. But Ruth had a very different anointing.

In Numbers 14:24 we come across a spirit that is much more like Ruth's spirit: "But because my servant Caleb has *a different spirit* and follows me wholeheartedly, I will bring him into the land he went to, and his descendants will inherit it" (NIV, emphasis added). If you remember the history of the Israelites, just before they entered the Promised Land (where Ruth and Naomi were going), Moses sent in spies to survey the land and come back with a report. The report would give the army of Israel what they needed to know so that they could have the right forces and weapons in place to take the territory.

When the spies returned, they gave this report:

> We went in to the land where you sent us; and it certainly
> does flow with milk and honey, and this is its fruit. But
> the people who live in the land are strong, and the cities
> are fortified (walled) and very large; moreover, we saw
> there the descendants of Anak [people of great stature and
> courage].... We are not able to go up against the people [of
> Canaan], for they are too strong for us.
> —NUMBERS 13:27–31

Caleb's take on the situation was different. With a few
words Caleb silenced the assembly of people and attempted
to raise the level of faith and expectancy: "Let us go up at
once and take possession of it; for we will certainly conquer
it" (Num. 13:30). But the people were leaning on their own
understanding and could not rest in God and know He had
already guaranteed their victory. They did not trust God with
their tomorrows, and their fear and anger were growing. Then
Joshua joined Caleb and they said:

> The land through which we passed as spies is an exceed-
> ingly good land. If the LORD delights in us, then He will
> bring us into this land and give it to us, a land which flows
> with milk and honey. Only do not rebel against the LORD;
> and do not fear the people of the land, for they will be our
> prey. Their protection has been removed from them, and
> the LORD is with us. Do not fear them.
> —NUMBERS 14:7–9

It is interesting that despite all the miracles God had per-
formed on their behalf, the Israelites thought Caleb's and
Joshua's thinking was so radical that they saw it as a threat to
their national security. The people were going to stone them until
the Lord Himself provided a sign showing that He approved of
their assessment. He confirmed that they had their faith placed
properly in His ability to guide and protect His people.

But the glory and brilliance of the LORD appeared at the
Tent of Meeting (tabernacle) before all the sons of Israel.

—NUMBERS 14:10

What is that saying? Where God guides, He provides?
Those with a different spirit like Caleb, Joshua, and Ruth
wholeheartedly believe that, and they will uproot their lives,
pursue the enemy, or take over territory at a moment's notice
if God gives the word. Those with a different spirit feel no
obligation to the crowd or to giving into their own wills. They
have decided to follow God wherever He leads. The outcome
is not for them to know at the moment. What they know and
rely on is that God has already secured for them a good future.
It is about following Him into it.

Orpah did not have this spirit, and neither did the other
spies nor the hundreds of thousands of Israelites who were
ready to stone Caleb and Joshua after they gave their report.
This "different spirit" is reserved for a select few who know
that they know God is in charge—no wavering, no waffling,
and no indecision—and can trust His sovereignty no matter
what things look like in the natural.

Naomi gave Ruth and Orpah a bad report:

Go back, my daughters, why should you go with me? Do
I still have sons in my womb that may become your husbands? Go back, my daughters, go, for I am too old to have
a husband. If I said I have hope, and if I actually had a husband tonight and even gave birth to sons, would you wait
until they were grown? Would you go without marrying?
No, my daughters; for it is much more difficult for me than
for you, because the LORD's hand has gone against me.

—RUTH 1:11–13

Sounds bleak. Naomi presented a picture of clear and present dangers that women at this time did not want to fall victim to. Without a family to provide for them, widows fell into abject poverty. Some starved to death. Some became beggars or prostitutes to avoid starvation. There was a high level of shame involved with this whole scenario. These were the giants Middle Eastern women faced during this time in history.

In considering this, Orpah turned back, but Ruth stayed. She was unbothered. She had already come to know the faithfulness of Naomi's God, so she restated her commitment: "Do not urge me to leave you or to turn back from following you; for where you go, I will go" (Ruth 1:16). This statement put an end to any further convincing Naomi might have tried, and the two women did not discuss it again.

Like Caleb and Joshua, Ruth had her resolve set to simply and faithfully follow God. She took literally the old church saying, "God said it. I believe it. That settles it." For some people of God those are just words. For those of a different spirit that phrase is representative of their entire lives with God. The endings to Caleb and Joshua's story and Ruth's at this juncture are different. The people of Israel did not take possession of the land at that time. As a matter of fact, God pronounced judgment against them for refusing to go into the land. He led them back into the wilderness. He withheld the blessings of the Promised Land from a whole generation of people who did not have the faith to see it. Caleb and Joshua were the only ones from that generation to survive the wilderness and finally take possession of the land. The people chose the wilderness over the Promised Land, the comfort zone over adventure. It is hard to believe that a lack of faith and fear of the future can cause even a wilderness to feel like a comfort zone.

Ruth, however, did not have a whole people to weigh in on

her decision. Naomi was the one who led and taught her by example, so as soon as Ruth said the word and established her loyalty, Naomi knew there was nothing more to do but to start the journey to Bethlehem. And so it was that the women came upon the land during the harvest season: "So Naomi returned from the country of Moab, and with her Ruth the Moabitess, her daughter-in-law. And they arrived in Bethlehem at the beginning of the barley harvest" (Ruth 1:22). I see this as God's blessing and approval of their faithful following of His leading into new and unfamiliar territory.

PRAYER THAT BUILDS FAITH

Jesus, You are the author and finisher of my faith. I believe that You have begun a good work in me and will bring me to a place of fulfillment and destiny. I am fully persuaded of Your promises over my life. My faith is not in the wisdom of men but in the power of God. I am a woman of faith. I walk by faith and not by sight. Lord, Your Word says that all things are possible to those who believe. Father, I believe You are God and a rewarder of those who diligently seek You. Cause me to see my life through Your eyes, the eyes of faith. Lord, I receive the gift of faith to do miraculous things for Your glory. I speak to the mountain, and the mountain must move. I believe that if I can see the invisible, I can do the impossible. I have taken the way of faith. I have kept Your decisions before me. I choose the path of faith. I will not allow doubt and unbelief to hinder my future. I am just, and I live by faith. Let me grow in my faith. I decree that Christ dwells in my heart by faith and I am rooted and grounded in His love.

PRAYER THAT BREAKS
ATTACHMENT TO THE COMFORT ZONE

Father, I believe that my comfort zone is the enemy of my future. I ask that You empower me to leave my comfort zone. Holy Spirit of God, give me courage to let go of every place of security and control. Deliver me from insecurity and fear that keeps me in a secure place. I let go of everything holding me back. I let go of intimidation and embrace courage. I let go of laziness and embrace diligence. I let go of average and embrace excellence. I let go of past mistakes and embrace new possibilities. I let go of bad habits and embrace new habits.

Lord, I ask You to change me. Lord, show me how to forget the things that are behind and reach forward to the things ahead. You said in Your Word that if we put our hands to the plow and look back, we are not worthy of Your kingdom. I set my eyes like a flint, looking to You, Lord, the author and finisher of my faith. I decree that I am moving on and moving up to the next level of my destiny. I break the spirit of apathy, complacency, and passivity. I decree that I am a water walker. Where You lead, I will follow. I will stop looking in the rearview mirror of life. I will embrace the new adventures You have for me in this quest to find and fulfill my destiny.

PRAYER THAT INVITES
A DIFFERENT SPIRIT

But because my servant Caleb has a different spirit and follows me wholeheartedly, I will bring him into the land he went to, and his descendants will inherit it.

—NUMBERS 14:24, NIV

I will follow the Lord wholeheartedly. As Ruth did, I will leave everything to serve the Lord and embrace His ways and His people. I will not allow race, economic status, or any other social factor define who I am. I have a different spirit. I will serve the generation before and leave a lasting legacy for the generations behind. I am a covenant woman. I will hear the voice of God clearly and follow His voice fully. I will not compromise the standards of the kingdom. I forget the things that are behind me and reach forward to the things ahead of me. I am a pioneer. I will not be afraid of difficult things. I will not be limited by cities, walls, or invisible fences erected by society. I will think outside the box. I will live a life that brings glory to the Lord and causes me to receive my inheritance. I decree that I am a woman of distinction. I carry the mark of distinction. I stand out in the crowd. I live my life separately and distinctly from the world.

Chapter 4

JUST CALL ME MARA

Looking diligently lest any man fail of the grace of God; lest any root of bitterness springing up trouble you, and thereby many be defiled.

—HEBREWS 12:15, KJV

IN THE FIRST chapter I mentioned three things women must be delivered from if we are going to walk in our destinies as modern-day Ruths: anger, fear, and bitterness. As we have seen thus far, Ruth operated with a different spirit, one of courage, resolve, and unshakeable faith in the future God had for her. Though Ruth had suffered great loss, we see that bitterness, anger, and fear were not found in her responses to God's movement in her life. Yet the Lord allows us to see bitterness manifested and healed through Naomi's experience. Her progression from insisting she be called Mara (Ruth 1:20), which means "bitter," to one who was blessed of the Lord (Ruth 4:14–15) is an example of how the Lord redeems and restores our losses and returns what the enemy has stolen.

The first thing we need to understand is that Elimelech led his family out of Judah—the Promised Land, the place that God had chosen for His people—to escape famine. The famine was God's judgment against the people of Israel for breaking covenant with Him and commingling with an idolatrous nation. Yet Elimelech led his family right to the place where God did not want His people to live. Elimelech had his mind set on doing all he could in the natural to save his family from disaster. But he missed one important thing—you cannot outrun the judgment of God.

One special thing about being in God and submitting to the process is that even when He is dealing with you and rebuking you, you are still under His authority and protection. Running away from, dodging, or rebelling against Him can cause you to move out from under His covering. In trying to save his family from the scarcity of famine, Elimelech actually moved his family out from under God's covering and exposed them to the enemy and further sin. Elimelech died (the Bible does not say how or why), and his sons married Moabite women. This was something God forbade His people to do—marry women who worshipped other gods. Some scholars believe that Elimelech was in rebellion and that his actions opened the door to the spirit of destruction, leading to his death and his sons' intermarriage and eventual deaths. Contrary to what Elimelech hoped his actions would produce, his family came out of Moab with less than what they entered with and less than what the people who endured the famine had as they stayed under God's divine covering.

It is not hard to see where Naomi's bitterness came from. Like some of us with our spouses, she may have known that Elimelech's actions were against God. I can imagine Naomi on moving day and every day leading up to it, working hard to be supportive and all the while perhaps knowing that leaving was going against what God said. It might have looked good, but it was not of God. She might have found a way to gently warn Elimelech, but she knew her place as wife and mother and his as husband, father, provider, and protector.

Part of the anointing coming on women in this season has

to do with women guarding their mouths and understanding and leading from our positions in the kingdom and in our families. According to Jewish custom, Naomi had a certain position in the family order. Think back on the chapter where I talked about how the lionesses organize themselves for the hunt. Naomi was faithful to her position and led from that place, so much so that despite the mess of her circumstances, her witness led one Moabite woman to the Lord.

The Next Right Move

Burdened with great grief at the loss of both her husband and two sons, Naomi's opportunities in a foreign land were greatly limited. At that time in Middle Eastern culture, an aging, poor widow had limited options for survival with no family around to support her. She had to think fast about her survival. What would be her next right move?

Even in extreme hardship the Lord is calling us to make sound decisions, and often decisions in seasons like this are destiny shapers. The next decision you make can lead you on a lengthy detour, or it could lead you on the fast track to reap your God-ordained harvest. Like what we have said of Ruth, Naomi chose well.

Naomi heard that the Lord had returned abundance to her people and decided to make the fifty-mile journey back home. I imagine that Naomi had many thoughts running through her mind about this decision. With such great losses behind her and what is revealed throughout the Bible about what God's people often thought about affliction, she must have felt that her family was being judged and corrected by God for leaving His covenantal protection. Perhaps she thought as the only living representative of her line she now had the responsibility to bear up under God's correction and right the wrong actions of her husband.

I pray that you can see this, beloved. Naomi was a mother in Israel. She came from a leading family of influence and knew well the ways of the Lord. She lived with her husband and served him with love and kindness the way Jewish women were taught. She was full of wisdom and was committed to God. She submitted herself to whatever correction the Lord had for her. By choosing to return home, she was essentially saying, "Lord, I repent for my family's collective decision to run from Your chastening. I humbly submit and recommit myself to Your ways and Your covenant. I desire to come under Your divine hand of protection. I desire to receive the portion You have for me—nothing more, nothing less."

She was not willing to sit in Moab, have a pity party, and waste away. No! With whatever strength she could muster— the level of grief she was experiencing causes some people to give up completely—she returned to the land of promise and provision.

My Name Is Not Naomi

After one daughter-in-law, Orpah, turned back, and with one unshakeable daughter-in-law at her side, Naomi made the fifty-mile journey to Bethlehem in Judah. The town was stirred by her return, which is what leads me to believe her family was a leading, influential, and perhaps wealthy family. A person of lower status returning to the city after a long absence would not have created such a stir as what Naomi caused. The Bible says that the people were shocked at the state Naomi was in as she entered the city—tattered, broken, poor, and desolate. This was not the Naomi they knew before the famine.

> When they arrived in Bethlehem, the whole city was
> stirred because of them, and the women asked, "Is this
> Naomi?" She said to them, "Do not call me Naomi (sweet-
> ness); call me Mara (bitter), for the Almighty has caused
> me great grief and bitterness. I left full [with a husband
> and two sons], but the LORD has brought me back empty.
> Why call me Naomi, since the LORD has testified against
> me and the Almighty has afflicted me?"
>   —RUTH 1:19–21

Though our usual conclusions about Naomi's statements in
the last part of this verse have led us to say that Naomi was
just bitter with God and blamed Him for her loss, I want to
challenge our thinking here. There are hidden strengths about
Naomi's relationship with God and her understanding of His
hand in her life. How could she have won Ruth's heart if she
was overcome by such a fragileness and immaturity in the spirit?
I do not think she could have. I do believe that Naomi was in
great distress, greatly grieved, and greatly hurt by the deaths
of the men she loved most dearly. But when we take her statements in the context of what I shared above, we see that Naomi
acknowledged the mighty hand of God had authority over her
affliction. Being a mother in Israel and a woman of deep and
abiding faith in the faithfulness of God, she had to have had
some level of peace and assurance that since it was the Lord's
hand guiding her through the affliction, she was going to be OK.

This happens to all of us. We can feel destitute and crushed
yet still have a mustard seed of faith somewhere crying out,
"Though He slay me, yet will I trust Him" (Job 13:15, NKJV).
And in our experience with the Lord, we know that it is never
the Lord's will to hurt or cause disaster in the lives of His
people. Our maturity helps us to see our roles in the hardships we face, and if it is not us, we know there is an adversary

who roams like a roaring lion, seeking whom he may devour, stealing, killing, and destroying (1 Pet. 5:8; John 10:10). Pushing everything on the Lord, both good and bad, was a common way the Old Testament people spoke about the happenings in life. It was all God. This is the place from which Naomi spoke. With the revelation we have today, we know that it was the decisions her husband made that caused the hand of the enemy to be activated in their lives.

The questions now are: How many of us can look back and see that this is not the perspective we took when it came to past hardships, hurts, losses, and disappointments? How many of us blame God for what happened in our lives? Can we look at ourselves soberly and see places where bitterness has caused us to be detoured from our destinies?

HEALING THE WATERS OF MARAH

Bitterness is a stronghold in many women's lives. We have a tendency to hold grudges against God and others and not realize how it holds us back from being all that God wants us to be. Some of us have gone through unmentionable loss, betrayals, and challenges, and the initial feelings of hurt, rejection, anger, and sadness were justified to a degree. But where are we now? Have we forgiven? Have we allowed the Lord to heal our hearts?

Naomi openly confessed her bitterness—"Call me Mara (bitter), for the Almighty has caused me great grief and bitterness" (Ruth 1:20)—and was healed. What do you need to confess to be brought to a place of deliverance and healing? The Bible says, "Therefore, confess your sins to one another [your false steps, your offenses], and pray for one another, that you may be healed and restored" (James 5:16). Naomi, mature in the Lord, let everyone know, "Yes, the Lord is dealing with me on some stuff. I am in His hands. I am broken now, but soon I will be healed and restored."

One of the first places in the Bible that we come across a word meaning "bitter," actually spelled *marah* in this instance, is also the same place we first learn of God as Jehovah Rapha, the Lord our Healer. In Exodus 15 the Israelites had just come out of bondage in Egypt. They saw the miraculous hand of the Lord deliver them from the hand of Pharaoh and drown him in the sea. They had been walking in the desert for three days and had not found water until they reached a spring, which was named Marah. But the water was not drinkable—it was bitter. Knowing the people would die without water, Moses prayed; the Lord showed him a tree close by and told him to throw the tree into the water to make it sweet or drinkable.

The word *marah* used in Exodus 15 means "bitter, change, be disobedient, disobey, grievously, provocation." It can also mean "to make bitter, to rebel, to provoke."[1] We do not want to walk in anger, disobedience, and rebellion, and that is how bitterness evolves if we do not get healed from it.

In his book *Unshakeable* my apostle and pastor John Eckhardt said, "There are so many different ways life can deal you a bitter hand. You have to guard your heart, because out of it flows the issues of life. You cannot allow your heart to become bitter or unforgiving."[2] He goes on to say this:

> If you allow unforgiveness and bitterness to get into your heart, you will be open to rebellion and will not walk in the blessing of God. So it is very important that we guard ourselves from unforgiveness, resentment, bitterness, anger, hatred, revenge, retaliation, and other such things. No matter what has happened to us, when we release things and forgive people we are also able to receive deliverance so

we can really walk in healing, health, prosperity, favor, and the blessing of God.[3]

This speaks directly to the heart of women seeking the Ruth anointing. The saying "Hell hath no fury like a woman scorned" is in some ways earned righteously. A woman can hold a grudge! But a woman can also be destroyed by a grudge and disqualified from a life of peace, blessing, and divine purpose. This is not the path we need to be on.

With salvation comes unlimited access to the healing and delivering power of God. There is no need for us to wallow in dangerous emotions such as anger, bitterness, revenge, and passive aggression. These behaviors hurt us more than they hurt those who hurt us in the first place. When you hold onto something, waiting for some kind of payback or revenge, it causes you to be stuck in that season of hurt and grief and minimizes your ability to move forward into the next season. You may be ministering, leading, mothering, and doing other things, but all of it is done with an undertone of bitterness. We will not experience the blessing and harvest that we hope for with bitterness in the way.

God is your healer. Confess your hurts, disappointments, and griefs to Him. He has already paid the price for all of it. I have heard from some that the tree Moses threw in the water represented the cross of Jesus Christ. He bore even your emotional hurts so that you could be set free from them. Naomi let the whole town know of the bitterness she was carrying. I don't know that you should do that, but you should confess it to a senior leader in your church, your mentor, or a trusted prayer partner, and find healing. And know this: in the midst of some of the deepest losses, hurts, or disappointments, God is still working out all things for your good. Naomi's story testifies to this:

> Blessed is the LORD who has not left you without a redeemer (grandson, as heir) today, and may his name become famous in Israel. May he also be to you one who restores life and sustains your old age; for your daughter-in-law, who loves you and is better to you than seven sons, has given birth to him....A son (grandson) has been born to Naomi.
>
> —RUTH 4:14–15, 17

What the Lord has for you next can look like this too. You can be restored sevenfold for the things the enemy has stolen from you, and it does not have to take a long time. Your submission to God and His process will catapult you into the next season.

> Afflictions will make great and surprising changes in a little time. May God, by his grace, fit us for all such changes, especially the great change![4]

THE BLESSING OF AFFLICTION

Many believe that God is good but not necessarily good to them. We believe that God is real, but we do not allow Him to be real in our lives. We often let mishap, misfortune, and mistakes get in the way of seeking, finding, and receiving God's love and mercy for our lives. Instead of letting the Lord come into those situations, we often keep Him out, never letting Him into our lives and never seizing the opportunity to get acquainted with Him.

We learn from Naomi that God's hand is on us even in affliction. And when we allow affliction to bring us to a place of humility where we can learn and grow to the next level of glory, that affliction was not in vain. Matthew Henry's commentary says this:

> It well becomes us to have our hearts humbled under humbling providences. When our condition is brought down our spirits should be brought down with it. And then our troubles are sanctified to us when we thus comport with them; for it is not an affliction itself, but an affliction rightly borne, that does us good.[5]

There is power and blessing in affliction. Romans 5:3–5 says, "Not only that, but we also rejoice in our sufferings, because we know that suffering produces perseverance; perseverance, character; and character, hope. And hope does not disappoint us, because God has poured out His love into our hearts through the Holy Spirit, whom He has given us" (BSB).

PRAYER THAT HEALS BITTERNESS

Lord, I ask that You create in me a clean heart and renew a righteous spirit within me. I repent of all bitterness, anger, and revenge. I forgive those who have caused me pain. I forgive those who have disappointed me. I release You, Lord, from anything that I think You owe me because I felt let down or did not understand Your timing. I know that You are faithful, that You never fail, and that You are always with me. I repent for blaming You for things I invited into my life because of disobedience, ignorance, or rebellion. I repent for blaming You for the things the enemy has done to sabotage Your perfect will for my life.

Right now, in the name of Jesus, I loose myself from all spirits of retaliation. I loose myself from all critical and cynical spirits that have entered my life through bitterness. I will no longer drink from the bitter waters of Marah, but I will trust in the Tree of Life to turn my sorrow into joy. I choose to love and believe in the goodness of the Lord that brings repentance.

Lord, remove the bitter taste of hurt, pain, loss, and rejection from my life. I choose to taste and see that You are good. Let your goodness fill my life. In Jesus's name, amen.

Chapter 5

BORN OUT OF ADVERSITY:
GOD'S DESIGN FOR
COVENANTAL CONNECTIONS

A friend loves at all times, and a brother is born for
adversity.

—PROVERBS 17:17

GOD IS SOVEREIGN, and He orders the moments of our lives.
Nothing is coincidental. God directs certain people into our
lives at pivotal times. They are the ones who move with us into
the next season, into the next job opportunity, or into the next
assignment on the road to our destinies. We were never meant
to journey through life alone, and some of the deepest, most
loyal relationships we have are formed out of enduring hard
times together. God is very intentional. Nothing catches Him
by surprise, and I believe that He connects us with others who
understand His timing and mandates in this season. We see
this in Ruth and Naomi's relationship. The essence of their
bond is captured in the words of Proverbs 17:17. Like He did
for Naomi and Ruth, God is helping us build true covenantal
relationships for the days ahead.

God-ordained friends who stick closer than a brother were
born for times of adversity. When we look at the partnership
God formed between these two women, we can see that they
would not have fulfilled their destinies alone. They did not just

say, "Let's be friends." These two women formed a covenant of friendship that will be the hallmark of modern-day Ruths in this hour. In order to better understand this, I am going to break down the elements of covenantal friendship.

DESTROYING THE "WOMEN CANNOT BE FRIENDS" MYTH

We all have either said or heard another woman say, "Oh, I don't get along with women," or "I have mostly male friends because women have too much drama." We say that like it is acceptable. Then reality TV shows such as the Real Housewives series further support the idea that women cannot have honest, loyal, and fulfilling friendships. In our society there can be betrayal, discord, confusion, and competition among women. But this is not God's plan for His daughters. This is the work of the enemy, who will use any means necessary to keep us from being unified for our godly purpose.

We all know it's true—when there is unity, a company of women is one of the most unstoppable forces on earth! When I want to get a job done, when I want to be uplifted and encouraged, when I need powerful prayer and intercession, when I need to go to war for my family, I know my sisters have my back. Confident, mature, and godly women have an ability to fight that no enemy on earth wants to come against. The Bible teaches that one can chase one thousand and two can put ten thousand to flight (Deut. 32:30).

The Ruth anointing is a direct and targeted attack against the belief that women cannot form lasting friendships. At its core the Ruth anointing manifests itself in relationships by displaying loyalty, perseverance, generosity, compassion, and humility. Women who embrace the Ruth anointing bring a pioneering spirit to their friendships that helps those they partner with endure hardship and forge new paths to abundance and prosperity. With this anointing there is an ability to find hope during tragedy through devotion to God. Modern-day Ruths carry a spirit of generosity that sustains hope through tragedy. They have a special gift to lift others up by their example and compassion. Their ability to consistently overcome temptations is contagious.

Modern-day Ruths give not only what is valuable and suitable to the relationship, but they also seek to do what is honorable. They have unselfish attitudes causing both people in their relationships to pour out affirmation, encouragement, and words of greatness. As selfishness sabotages friendships, the Ruth anointing quickly causes women to promote the other person over themselves. Ruths are mindful of the need to consistently protect their relationships by always being faithful with words, attitudes, and actions. They champion and protect the interests of those in covenant with them. The rivalry, selfishness, and antagonism sometimes associated with women have no place in covenant relationships. The main mode of operation of modern-day Ruths is all about self-sacrifice for the good of others.

With their classic resolute style, Ruths have a devotion to God that gives them the power to faithfully endure the seasons of friendship. There are times when the strong must bear the infirmities of the weak. Ruth did not stop to think twice; she knew that she needed to go with Naomi to Bethlehem and do whatever it took to help Naomi survive. Naomi was an older woman who could not work and needed a family to provide for her. Ruth committed to being Naomi's family. In Galatians 6:2 we read, "Carry one another's burdens and in this way you will fulfill the requirements of the law of Christ [that is, the law of

Christian love]." And Romans 15:1–2 says, "Now we who are strong [in our convictions and faith] ought to [patiently] put up with the weaknesses of those who are not strong, and not just please ourselves. Let each one of us [make it a practice to] please his neighbor for his good, to build him up spiritually."

These verses are the backbone for the conduct of modern-day Ruths in friendships. For them, being placed in relationship with others is neither a coincidence nor a casual connection. Friendships are few for women with the Ruth anointing, but they are powerful and strategic. They are covenants.

RUTH AND A COVENANT OF LOYALTY

Loyalty can be defined as "a feeling of devotion, duty, or attachment to somebody or something," or being "firm and not changing in your friendship with or support for a person or an organization, or in your belief in your principles."[1] Loyalty is about unwavering commitment to another person. If you are loyal to someone, you are essentially making these two declarations:

1. My loyalty gives you my steadfastness. I am here for good or for bad. I am not leaving; you are stuck with me.

2. My loyalty gives you my love. I do not do this out of obligation but because of a commitment of love to you.

A commitment of loyalty is much like a covenant agreement. Defined as "a usually formal, solemn, and binding agreement…a promise within a contract for the performance or nonperformance of a particular act,"[2] covenant is the basis of humankind's relationship to God. The whole structure of our walk with God is based on covenant. Upon entering the family of God, we enter in to the Abrahamic covenant established in Genesis 12:1–3, when God committed His sovereign loyalty to Abraham and his seed, which we are grafted into by salvation through Jesus Christ (Rom. 11:17). The stipulations of the covenant—both the blessings when the covenant is honored and the curses when the covenant is broken—are listed in Deuteronomy 7. We break His covenant through disobedience and by rejecting Him as Lord of our lives. God is always faithful to His part of the covenant. He never wavers in His loyalty to His people. Our faithfulness, on the other hand, does waver. But thank God for deliverance, grace, and mercy!

Covenant, therefore, requires loyalty from both parties with the purpose to guarantee that the relationship will last and remain healthy. The covenant itself is a series of words that are spoken to define the nature of the relationship and the principles of commitment to it. When covenant is the foundation for relationships, the possibility of maintaining permanence and stability is greatly enhanced. When you are aligned with God's covenant, you will experience peace, protection, prosperity, and favor. You experience stability in your life and relationship with God. Tracing the history of the people of Israel, you will find that they experienced great instability, disease, attack from enemies, and more because they did not hold up their end of the covenant agreement. Still, God in His great love always rescued them and restored them back to right standing with Him.

The relationship between Ruth and Naomi reflects the faithful love of God offered to Israel and to us in the gift of covenant. Ruth, leaning in to the call of her destiny and seeing Naomi's need for family, was the initiator of this covenant.

RUTH'S SEVENFOLD
COVENANTAL DECLARATION

Ruth 1:16–17 contains one of the most powerful statements of commitment and loyalty in the Bible. It is the manifesto of women who operate with a spirit like Ruth. Within this sevenfold declaration are demonstrations of the power of decision mingled with determination. These statements are symbolic of a treaty or covenant of devotion. Her declarations show strong resolve infused with covenant love. They give us a glimpse into heart of a woman who set her heart to express compassion and loyalty. Let's look at the seven statements in Ruth 1:16–17 (NLT) one by one.

1. "Wherever you go, I will go" represents a willingness to move forward.

2. "Wherever you live, I will live" indicates willingness to relocate and change from a familiar environment.

3. "Your people will be my people" marks a redefinition of identity (i.e., a changed name and nature). She renounced her Moabite roots of false worship so that she could worship the true and living God.

4. "Your God will be my God" sets forth a receiving of salvation and redemption.

5. "Wherever you die, I will die" signifies an unshakeable commitment to family.

6. "And there I will be buried" indicates the knowledge that nothing is as final and complete as the grave. Similar to Esther's "If I perish, I perish," Ruth pledged her life in service to God and His people.

7. "May the LORD punish me severely if I allow anything but death to separate us" communicates an
   intimate understanding of the fear of the Lord.

These words will live and breathe in the actions of modern-
day Ruths. You will know them by their fruit, by their actions,
because there will not be much said after they have committed.
Women with an anointing akin to Ruth will carry a heart of
humility and sacrifice. Committed to the best interest and
well-being of others, they will be determined to use their gifts
and talents to serve them. And while committed to others,
they will be even more devoted to the Lord.

The story of Ruth and Naomi demonstrates the power of
mutual commitment between two women. When we choose
to form a covenantal friendship, we surrender ourselves to
unconditionally loving another person and develop a relationship that attests to the faithfulness and goodness of God.

Our society advertises the appeal and success of women
who are interested in themselves and do not care about the
needs of others, but I believe Christian women should break
this mold. We must lead by example. There is a generation
of women who will epitomize what it means to be a friend.
Society is full of women longing for friendship, for relationship, and we can draw them in as we return to how the Bible
defines and describes *friendship*.

> Faithful are the wounds of a friend [who corrects out of
> love and concern], but the kisses of an enemy are deceitful
> [because they serve his hidden agenda].
>
> —PROVERBS 27:6

This is My commandment, that you love and unselfishly
seek the best for one another, just as I have loved you. No

one has greater love [nor stronger commitment] than to lay
down his own life for his friends.

—JOHN 15:12–13

And above all things have fervent love for one another, for
"love will cover a multitude of sins." Be hospitable to one
another without grumbling. As each one has received a gift,
minister it to one another, as good stewards of the mani-
fold grace of God.

—1 PETER 4:8–10, NKJV

I have observed that when we enter covenant relationships, we are supernaturally affected by them. Our relationships change us. We can enter relationships that can change
us for good or evil. The Bible tells us, "As iron sharpens iron,
so one man sharpens [and influences] another" (Prov. 27:17). I
believe the Lord used Ruth to influence Naomi to hope and
believe again. I believe their covenant relationship allowed love
to blossom in Naomi's heart again after such great loss. Many
times the Lord will use people and covenant relationships to
return us to our first love, to fill us with hope for the future,
and to help us feel alive again.

DESTINED TO BE A COVENANT FRIEND

It was not until I studied Ruth's name that I saw how God
purposed her life from the foundation of the earth. Ruth was
destined to be a covenant friend. Her name means "friendship." It probably comes from a root word meaning "friend,"
"neighbor," or "companion."[3]

Our destinies were established at the foundation of the
earth as well. And though the names our parents gave us may
not mean "friend," we are still commanded by God to love
others as He loves us. We express the heart of a covenant

friend by being with others through adversity, by being loyal, and by always having their best interests at heart. People are not always easy to love, so we cannot think that love for others is mustered up within ourselves. It is the love of God "poured out in our hearts by the Holy Spirit" (Rom. 5:5, NKJV). The level of commitment and loyalty modern-day Ruths express in humble service to others is supernatural. Our commitment to see others restored to their purposes and destinies will cause us to walk right into our own. Love begets love. Favor begets favor.

THE POWER OF
COVENANTAL PARTNERSHIPS

There is a flow when true friends are working in unison. There are things you know the other person needs without them being said. You can be free to direct a friend to a task, resource, or solution, knowing that she understands you have her best interest at heart. You can freely seek out a true friend when you need help or guidance, ready to receive her wisdom.

Once in Bethlehem, their loyalty to each other declared, Ruth and Naomi operated in a similar flow. The two women got down to the business of providing for their basic needs and devising a plan to redeem Elimelech's estate. They each had a role to play, and if they did not stay in their positions, the whole plan could have unraveled.

Whenever the Lord wants a task accomplished, He creates partnerships and teams. An acronymic version of the word *team* is "together everyone accomplishes more." I believe that this is the appointed time for women to become covenant members of strategic teams that are assigned to take back territory for the kingdom of God. In *The Deborah Anointing* I point out four keys to effective teamwork:

1. Honor—showing respect for team members' positions, authority, gifts, and callings

2. Purpose—team members' awareness of the "point at issue," the specific reason we are all here

3. Measure of rule—team members not going beyond the reach of their authority

4. Diversity of gifts and administrations—submitting and aligning with the established order[4]

In examining Ruth and Naomi's movement as a unified team, we see that all of these factors were securely in place. Naomi's position was the older, wiser woman, one who knew the mores of the culture, and she served as a type of the Holy Spirit. Ruth was a foreigner and the younger woman; she knew her place, received Naomi's wisdom about the culture, and trusted her instruction when it came to securing their provision and the rights to the land that belonged to their family.

Knowing our position is important and is connected with our victory in many areas. As women of God, we are dangerous to the devil when we know our positions. Therefore, I am challenging women everywhere: Find your place, and be secure in it. Do what you have been called to do, and do it well.

Some people are called to be in the forefront. Some are not. Some are going to be on the side to support. Some will be in the background. We need to be comfortable with our callings. I have already talked about the significance of encountering the God of your call, and I repeat it here. Meeting the God of your call and receiving from Him a visitation around your purpose will give you permission to be yourself. How many hats do you wear? I am giving you permission to take some of them off. For maximum fruitfulness, you are only responsible to be in the position God has called you to.

PRAYERS FOR COVENANT RELATIONSHIPS

Lord, I ask You to make me into a covenant friend. I believe that one can chase a thousand and two can put ten thousand to flight. In covenant friendships there is exponential power to accomplish more in the kingdom. Lord, bring women into my life with whom I can agree in faith. I believe that there is power in agreement. Agreement and unity attracts Your presence. I ask You to bring divine connections and friendships into my life. I believe two are better than one. I break the spirit off my life that causes me to try to do things on my own. Send loyal women into my life, women who will love me for who I am and not what I can give them. Lord, Your Word says there is no greater love than for a man to lay down his life for his friends. I ask that You would make me into a selfless friend. Teach me how to serve others and place others' needs before my own.

❧

Lord, release a new expression of teamwork among women. Let women understand that together we can accomplishment more for Your glory. I break the spirit of discord and confusion among women. We will rise up and declare those things we can do together. These are the days when every woman will find her rank and column in the army of the Lord—no pushing or competing, but supporting and encouraging our sisters in their destinies.

Chapter 6

BARRIER BREAKER

But we do not belong to those who shrink back and are destroyed, but to those who have faith and are saved.
—HEBREWS 10:39, NIV

IN THE INTRODUCTION to this book we identified the pioneering spirit as one of the key traits of the Ruth anointing. A pioneer is "a person or group that originates or helps open up a new line of thought or activity or a new method or technical development; one of the first to settle in a territory."[1] Through her decisive and resolute action, Ruth originated and opened up a new method and line of thought concerning what it meant to be a daughter-in-law and to be in a covenant friendship with another woman. This concept alone is something the enemy uses against women. He whispers to us that we cannot get along, that other women are in competition with us, or that other women hope the worst for us. Instead of giving in to these ideas, modern-day Ruths will remember that we are not fighting against flesh and blood and remember who the real enemy of our souls is. The devil knows that if we were to unify, we could turn the world upside down. Ruths know the value of unity and will climb over or break down every barrier to achieve it.

As the definition above points out, pioneering Ruths will be the first to settle new territories. This territory can be spiritual, physical, emotional, cultural, or relational. By the very essence of their unique natures, Ruths break the barriers that stand in the way of their God-ordained destinies. A barrier is anything that blocks or stops you from getting to where you are going. The dictionary defines it as "something material that blocks or is intended to block passage; a natural formation or structure that prevents or hinders movement or action; something immaterial that impedes or separates."[2] Material barriers such as a physical wall, closed door, or highway barricade are easier to see and therefore tear down, go over, or go through. But the immaterial ones are the ones that have us locked in place—mental and emotional barriers such as fear, unforgiveness, and doubt, and limiting beliefs such as poverty and victim mentalities. Through the story of Ruth, the immaterial barriers revealed themselves as she overcame national and ethnic, familial, gender, class and economic, religious, and geographic boundaries and limitations to get to her promised place in God. Ruth gives us an example to follow as we seek to overcome similar roadblocks.

BREAKING THROUGH NATIONAL, ETHNIC, OR RACIAL BARRIERS

At the time that the Bible picks up on Ruth's story, we immediately come to understand that she was in transition between her old life in Moab and a new life in Bethlehem, Judah. We can also see through her declaration—"Your people will be my people, and your God, my God. Where you die, I will die, and there I will be buried" (Ruth 1:16–17)—that Ruth understood what leaving her land and people to join another meant. She was an immigrant. Her nationality was different from the nationality of those she was going to join. She kept different social customs. She dressed differently. She spoke a different language. She was of a different ethnicity and may have even been of a different race and skin color. She was like many of the millions of people who immigrate to various nations seeking opportunity and a new life. Some, like Ruth, plan to shed the citizenship of their old homeland to take up a new citizenship in their new land. And just like modern immigrants, Ruth may have experienced social, ethnic, or racial discrimination, stereotyping, or judgment just because she was different.

Moab and Israel had a long history as geographic neighbors. Sometimes they were at war; other times they were at peace. Moab was an idol-worshipping nation named after the son of Lot and his eldest daughter.[3] They were the kind of people God forbade Israel from intermingling with because of His covenant with them. (See Deuteronomy 7.)

So now we read that Ruth made a declaration to put aside all the years of rejection, exclusion, segregation, and judgment she may have experienced as a result of being a citizen of a nation Israel could not interact with; she decided to join them. This is a bold move. Not only did Ruth decide to lay aside any prejudice or bias she may have had, she also moved to a new land knowing that the Israelites might not do the same for her.

As a foreigner, Ruth came into Bethlehem a poor, unemployed widow. She had to find work and provision immediately for herself and her mother-in-law. This could not have been easy. Can you imagine the looks she got as she moved about the town with her Moabite clothes and jewelry, her Moabite hair and makeup, and her Moabite ways? Can you hear the whispers and see the stares of the townspeople? Did a mother grab her child and bring her close as Ruth walked by? Did another woman secure the strap of her purse as Ruth caught her eye?

If you are part of a minority or marginalized group in your community, maybe these scenarios are familiar. But just as is characteristic of modern-day Ruths, our ancient model set her mind to do what she needed to do and did not shrink back. A stranger in a strange land, Ruth boldly and unwaveringly broke through the barriers and limitations Jewish society placed on her. She committed herself to her new God, and she went to work doing all her hands could find to do. Ruth had no sense of entitlement and no expectation of fair and equal treatment; she did not wait for someone to pity her condition and give her any handouts. Because of her diligence, faithfulness, and kindness to her mother-in-law, she caught the eye of a wealthy man and was granted favor. She went from gleaner in the field to owner of the field in no time.

Beloveds, God is accelerating our season of promotion. We will work diligently, and it will not be too long before we receive the favor of God over all we put our hands to do. Favor is when someone uses a position of influence to bless you. We will not be limited by race, ethnicity, or nationality because we will take on a new kingdom identity. We will not be ethnocentric; we will be Christocentric—Christ-centered.

Ruth did not care what she would face. When she made the declaration, "Your people shall be my people," that was it. Even while confident in who she was—different and unique from the people of Israel—she was determined to work and assimilate to the culture around her. She did not come in thinking she was better than or less than the people of Israel. In essence she said to Naomi, "I will find my place among your people." She did not care what cultural differences were there. God made special allowances for people like Ruth, people who committed to worship and serve Him only. He made room in His covenant—and in His family line—for her. She was not an Israelite by birth, but she became one in spirit.

Ruths of today will carry in them a distinction, a unique factor, which sets them apart from all those around them. They will dress differently, look differently, talk differently, and have a different level of confidence that causes them to stand out and their gifts to be seen by great men. God is calling modern-day Ruths to pioneer racial harmony in the earth. God is releasing a boldness upon women to cross any perceived color barriers and find strategic ways to promote healing and unity among races. This begins with examining ourselves, our convictions, the things that define us, and the truth we stand for. We must make the Word of God the final authority in our lives—not our feelings, not what our parents may have taught, but what Scripture commands. The gospel commands us to pursue racial harmony. We must rise above the racial barriers within and without. We must ask the Holy Spirit to give us practical ways we can love and serve our diverse neighbors as we pursue racial unity through the gospel. The Holy Spirit will give us the courage to lead prayer initiatives that focus on racial unity to bring racial healing in these racially divided times and beyond. As we do these things, we will offer up fervent prayers for God to unify all people in Christ and to eliminate prejudice through the truth of the gospel. We must pray that God will grant us wisdom and courage to be conduits of racial healing. I believe nothing is impossible with our God.

BREAKING THROUGH RELIGIOUS BARRIERS

Ruth was from an idolatrous nation. The national deity of the Moabites was Chemosh, who was also a god of the Ammonites. Although Israel actually ended up worshipping Chemosh during the reign of Solomon, Ruth (Solomon's great-great-grandmother) would have been looked down upon because of what the Israelites knew of her people's religious practices.[4] The Lord made it clear that they were to have nothing to do with idol worshippers. (See Deuteronomy 7.) Any legalistic Israelite would have given Ruth a hard time. But Ruth made it known to Naomi and all those who might have asked that Naomi's God was her God. Furthermore, Ruth got to work proving that this was her new truth. By letting her actions speak louder than her words, Ruth proved her commitment among Naomi's kinsmen, and they sheltered and protected her. She is an example of true repentance and salvation to the point of being worthy to be married to one of the elders in the community. Modern-day Ruths will not allow religious paradigms to stop them from doing everything the Lord has called them to do in the kingdom.

BREAKING THROUGH FAMILY
AND GENERATIONAL BARRIERS

Being born into a people whom Israel wanted nothing to do with, Ruth may have grown up with all kinds of limiting thoughts. From the perspective of the Israelite nation, Ruth the Moabite was born on the wrong side of the tracks. She was a part of a people who should be shunned, rejected, and excluded from anything Israel was doing. So when Elimelech and his family with two single sons came into town and one showed interest in her, she may have wondered what people would think. Perhaps she was tired of being discriminated against and cordoned off to a certain place among the two nations. As I mentioned in an earlier chapter, Elimelech was the head of an affluent Jewish family. He was a leader in Bethlehem. But then Ruth's husband died. Can you imagine the grief she felt? It was more than just losing a husband; maybe she was also losing a long-desired social status and security for her future. Ruth fell from a place of prominence as the wife of a wealthy and revered family to being at the bottom rung of society as a penniless widow. Her family and others in the town must have had a field day tormenting her the many versions of "I told you so," or "I told you that life was never meant for us," or "They will never see you as equal to them."

Limiting thoughts like these create mental and spiritual bondages in our minds that lead us to believe the worst about ourselves. We even start to speak over ourselves what we have heard our family say—and we begin to behave as if these things are true. This is part of the cycle of generational curses. I believe that Ruth's declaration in Ruth 1:16–17 was the bondage breaker over all of the generational lies she had come to believe. It was her "enough is enough" moment. Decisiveness and resolution can be the beginning of breakthrough. The moment we say, "No more!" the chains begin to fall off.

Ruth said, "Do not urge me to leave you or to turn back from following you" (Ruth 1:16). In other words, "Mother Naomi, don't give me that sad story one more time. You will not convince me to turn back. I have nothing to go back to. I am moving forward with you and your God. Respectfully, this is the end of the discussion."

Ruth saw something greater for herself on the horizon. The limited life and the limited people she had known in Moab were not going to determine the expanse of the life she had ahead of her. Her decision to move forward broke generations of curses that had been warring for her destiny. I can imagine Ruth thinking, "Not today, devil. You will not steal, kill, or destroy what is mine anymore!"

The Ruth anointing will not be held back by anything that is not from God. No curses, no race, no ethnicity, no gender—nothing will keep us from living in the fullness of our call and destiny.

BREAKING THROUGH CLASS
AND ECONOMIC BARRIERS

Research shows that women suffer higher rates of poverty than men. According to US Census Bureau data released in 2015, the poverty rates for women are substantially higher than the rates for men. The overall poverty rate is 3.8 percentage points higher for women than for men, and the difference in the poverty rate among those over the age of sixty-five is even higher, with nearly one in five women who are over sixty-five and live alone living in poverty.[5] We see this played out in the Book of Ruth, but Ruth did not wait for any governmental agency or nonprofit organization to advocate for her economic well-being. She made a decision to go to work. She took the initiative to ask Naomi if it was OK for her to work among a foreign people. Ruth took the initiative and went from being a poor widow to being a business owner. I believe that God blessed her initiative and her willingness to work by directing her to Boaz's land, and I believe that God will similarly bless modern-day Ruths for their initiative and willingness by directing their steps. Ruth 2:3 says Ruth happened to come to the field that belonged to Boaz, but nothing just happens when you commit to the ways of the Lord. This is a strong indication of the leading and guiding of the Lord into her purpose. Ruth's extraordinary commitment to the Lord caused Him to do some extraordinary things in her life.

In this season God is raising up Ruths who will break the barrier of poverty. They will use what is in their hands and be determined, faithful, and diligent. Ruths are the hardest workers in the room. The quality and quantity of their work will draw the attention of people around the world. They will earn every promotion and ounce of favor given, and in turn they will be the catalyst for breaking the spirit of poverty that has plagued their families for generations. Ruths break through class and economic barriers by working on behalf of others. They do not selfishly work for personal wealth and privilege. As Ruth worked because she cared for Naomi, modern-day Ruths will work thinking of all those who will benefit from their gifts and talents. While they will also benefit, they know that their work and the success they achieve are not about them. Modern-day Ruths will demonstrate the love of God in powerful, earthshaking ways. They will become great humanitarians who will bring salvation by creating programs and institutions to help do good to widows and orphans.

Breaking Through Gender Barriers

Gender discrimination is still alive and thriving, but it is more covert and subtle. Fighting discrimination that manifests in hidden perceptions requires a weapon that is both powerful and effective: confidence. We can break through stereotypes by knowing and believing the truth that we were fearfully and wonderfully made to be different, not less, and by laughing at gender barriers as we overcome them, knowing beyond the shadow of a doubt that women have what it takes to break through for their families and communities and lead them to fulfilling God's plans and purposes. We can overcome.

I cannot state this enough: Ruth was a woman, and not just a woman but also a widow. Women were already considered lower than men, but a poor widow was even lower than that. There were just a few roles her society had decided were good enough for women in her position—beggar or prostitute. Ruth did not even entertain those options. Shortly after the women's arrival in Bethlehem, Ruth was already thinking how she would provide. In Ruth 2:2 we read, "And Ruth the Moabitess said to Naomi, 'Please let me go to the field and glean among the ears of grain after one [of the reapers] in whose sight I may find favor.'" She had already scoped out what she could do, so she got herself together, rolled up her sleeves, and got to work. She was not thinking about being a woman. She had to do what she had to do.

It was not long before news of Ruth's kindness toward her mother-in-law and work ethic broke through the ranks and reached the owner of the field. Then Boaz asked the servant in charge of the reapers, "Whose young woman is this?" (Ruth 2:5). When he discovered who she was and what she had done, he granted her safety and favor above the other reapers: "I have been made fully aware of everything that you have done for your mother-in-law since the death of your husband, and how you have left your father and mother and the land of your birth, and have come to a people that you did not know before. May the LORD repay you for your kindness, and may your reward be full from the LORD, the God of Israel, under whose wings you have come to take refuge" (Ruth 2:11–12). In the midst of a male-dominated society God restored and redeemed the lives of Naomi and Ruth, causing them to be an intricate part of history.

The news of your kindness and hard work will break through the ranks. You might have been held back for reasons beyond your control, but they are not beyond God's control and you will suddenly be recognized and promoted. As a modern-day Ruth you are a shining example of the transforming power of God and His goodness toward women. He has anointed you to be a barrier breaker. The anointing of Ruth is upon you and you will break through!

How to Break Through

My daughter, Eboni, is my favorite example of a modern-day Ruth. She is a barrier breaker. She broke the barrier of sight and has traveled to twenty-three nations. She trains and mentors teams of young people and then takes them to the nations. Like Ruth, she even married interracially. As a female leader, she has broken the barriers of gender and race and is excelling in her gifts. One thing I taught her is that we must change the narrative of her story. Yes, she was born with a visual impairment, but that will not determine who she is and what she can accomplish. Our motto for her life has been that she would see what she could of the world with her natural eyes, but she would change the world through the eyes of her heart. We are believing God for total deliverance and healing in her sight, but as her mother I did not allow this misfortune to become a part of the family. I trained her to determine what God called her to be and go after it with all of her heart. Modern-day Ruths will be women of vision and passion to fulfill their purpose.

Eboni and other women like her fully exhibit the Ruth anointing in their everyday lives, unhindered by societal expectations. I have shared some of the barriers that Ruth and her modern-day counterparts face, and I also gave ideas on the tools and attributes Ruths need to break through those barriers. I want to highlight them here for you so that you do not miss what you need to accomplish all that God has for you.

1. Decisiveness—a catalyst for breakthrough

The first thing that jumps out at me when I think about Ruth is her decisiveness. She confidently exercised her power of choice and decision. I firmly believe that this was the catalyst for Ruth's barrier-breaking power. She did not vacillate between two opinions. This is also indicative of her pioneering spirit. Pioneers make hard and risky choices with expedience. They do not stay in the valley of decision long. They have a sense of what needs to be done and do it. They are aware of the potential persecution or challenges that may come as a result of their decisions to engage, but they are confident and resolute in their decisions. Think of those who fought for civil rights in America and around the world. Many of them faced death, yet they did not waver in their commitment to see fair and equal treatment for all people.

Barrier breakers have an instinct to be different and to be difference makers, as T. D. Jakes points out in his book *Instinct*.[6] They cannot do anything else but break outside of the mold. God puts this in them. He knows us all, and He knows what He has called us to do. He also knows what we will do with the decisions we make. It is innate in us. This barrier-breaking, pioneering spirit is what He formed in us as we were in our mothers' wombs.

2. Faith—a mountain mover

Faith breaks barriers and activates the supernatural. It is heaven's currency. If you want God to move on your behalf, petition Him in faith, then move with Him in faith, and receive His favor. The Bible says that without faith it is impossible to please God (Heb. 11:6). When God delights in you, no barrier on earth can stop you. God delights in those who obey and fear Him.

Faith propels you forward. It compels you to engage. Hebrews 10:38 says, "The just shall live by faith; but if anyone draws back, my soul has no pleasure in him" (NKJV). I love verse 39: "We are not of those who draw back" (NKJV)—we lean in, we step up, and we do not turn back. Our faith in action shows us to be women who are engaged and accept the challenge to break through every barrier we face so that the next generation can be better positioned for what they set out to do.

Faith is confidence in God's power working in us. And when we exercise that faith, we will have everything we ask for. What was once hard is now easy. What was impossible is now possible. Jesus said, "With God all things are possible" (Matt. 19:26). We can even move mountains. All we need to prosper in our call is granted and is yes and amen through Jesus Christ.

Even though the Holy Spirit was not mentioned at all in the Book of Ruth, we can see Him leading Ruth every step of the way. Whatever she needed, He worked it out in the natural and it came to her. This power is even more available to you who are the very temple of the Spirit of God. When you pray, your prayers will avail much (James 5:16). When you ask the Lord for wisdom, He will give it to you without limit (James 1:5). When you pray in faith, the sick will be healed, broken hearts will be mended, the hungry will be fed, and the naked will be clothed. Whatever you ask of the Lord will be given to you when you ask in faith. I like the way the New International Version of the Bible translates a portion of Matthew 15:28; just as Jesus said to the Canaanite woman, He says to you, "Woman, you have great faith! Your request is granted."

3. Confidence—the core of a new women's movement

If you have been watching the news, you have seen reports of women marching for various reasons and advocating for policies about issues that affect them, such as equal pay, domestic violence, and paid family leave. While many of these issues are important, I believe that God is instigating a new women's movement—one that works in the heart of women first then extends out to other women, our families, our communities, and finally the world. The core of this women's movement is the confidence we develop as we work in tandem with other women. Women need deliverance from doubt, insecurity, intimidation, and inferiority complexes. Women need to be empowered to find our identity and love who we are.

We need a women's movement that will encourage us to forge better relationships with other women, along with one that promotes women excelling in careers, economic literacy, and entrepreneurial developments. A women's movement like this can only thrive when its participants are armed with supernatural confidence. That is why I call this new women's movement a movement of confidence.

The word *confidence* is defined as "the feeling or belief that one can rely on someone or something; firm trust; the state of feeling certain about the truth of something; a feeling of self-assurance arising from one's appreciation of one's own abilities or qualities."[7] Words associated with confidence are *trust, belief, faith, credence,* and *conviction.*[8]

In their book *The Confidence Code* Katty Kay and Claire Shipman write about how women's wiring is more toward competence than it is for confidence.[9] Women want everything perfectly lined up, and when it is not, our level of confidence goes down. Women tend to worry because all the pieces are not there, which causes us to doubt ourselves. We feel more confident when everything is in order first.

But many times in life every detail or scenario is not there or worked out. We must learn how to move forward and not hold back because we do not have all of the pieces in place. Most of the time we do not know how things are going to turn out, but we can be confident that God can lead us through it.

Biblical confidence

The kind of confidence I am talking about is God confidence, a firm knowing that God put in you all that you need to succeed. The Bible says, "Do not cast away your confidence, which has great reward" (Heb. 10:35, NKJV). In other words, do not look on confidence as something of little value. Confidence comes with great rewards. Confidence is a mantle we can embrace. It is like a cloak we can put on and take off. Confidence is a choice—either put it on and reap the rewards or cast it aside, devaluing its effect in our lives. The rewards of confidence are endurance, consistency, steadfastness, and the ability to summon courage and resolution in difficult situations with a strength of mind that actively resists defeat. This is the confidence God gives. God confidence is not arrogance or bossiness. It is not perfectionism. Perfectionism is fear-based and hinders everything. Confidence is wholly based on our reliance on God's power to work in and through us.

The missing piece

Sometimes after all the worrying for every detail to fall in place, the only missing piece is confidence. Women are brilliant. We work hard, study, train, practice, and learn the ins and outs of everything set before us. Yet we are also the ones who will know more than everyone at the table and still feel unsure. There is a spiritual glass ceiling put there by the devil, and if we do not have confidence, we will bump up against it every time. Insecurity, fear, shame, and mind-sets put a limit on how far we go. If we do not break through those things, we will not be successful. Do you remember the verse, "We are not of those who draw back," or as another translation puts it, "We are not of those who shrink back" (Heb. 10:39, NKJV, NASB)? God has already shattered that glass ceiling, and He has created a space for us in the earth. Do not shrink back. Instead, lean in.

How confidence is developed

There are five ways we can develop the confidence we need to break through barriers of every kind:

1. Seek out a mentor. When we come together to encourage each other, provide constructive feedback, and exchange ideas, opportunities, and resources, we help to secure each other's future. There was a point when Naomi woke up and stepped outside of her own pain to help Ruth. We can see the light bulb go off in Ruth 2:20 when she realizes her daughter-in-law has a good thing going and God's favor is on her: "Then Naomi said to her daughter-in-law, 'Blessed be he of the LORD, who has not forsaken His kindness to the living and the dead!' And Naomi said to her, 'This man is a relation of ours, one of our close relatives'" (NKJV). This was when Naomi rose up out of her grief and began to instruct Ruth on what to do to make sure she was positioned well for their collective advancement.

   This is what mentors do. They see something special and believe you are the one to bring it out and multiply it. They see into your ideas and vision and know that you are onto something. Believing in your vision, mentors give you insight and strategy. Mentors will speak faith to you when you are doubting. They see who you are. Initially they have more faith in you than you have in yourself, and you are able to lean on that when things get hard and confusing. They are the ones who have walked through it before you have. This is the dynamic we see in Ruth and Naomi's relationship. As the Bible points out in Titus 2:3–5, older women are to lead the younger women.

In a mentoring relationship there should be no competition. The mentor provides a safe place for other women to be vulnerable, a place where they can get help and be uplifted, corrected, advised, and strengthened. Oftentimes women function as the caregivers, but in a mentoring relationship we have a chance to receive care.

2. Use our gifts. When we identify and use our gifts, we begin to prove to ourselves our own value. We begin to see what we did with our own hands to produce what once existed only in our minds. Using what God put in our hands and seeing it become something tangible is a confidence booster. Some people live on the sidelines of life and miss out on the chance to see what they can do and what they are made of. For those with the Ruth anointing, using our gifts is something that will quickly build our confidence and cause us to desire to do even more.

3. Do not stay idle; do something. When Ruth had every excuse to just lie there and die or have a pity party—she had lost everything!—she rose up and said, "I am not going to just sit here and die." In that moment of decision she not only pledged herself to actively provide for her and Naomi's new life, she also broke through another barrier—the barrier of grief. Anytime you need to be broken out of a rut such as disappointment, loss, or heavy-heartedness,

look out beyond yourself. Whom can you serve?
Who needs help or encouragement? Do not sit
there and be idle. You will find the joy of the Lord,
and confidence in Him will return to you when
you reach out to bless others.

4. Stay engaged. Ruth may have thought, "My life
   did not work out in Moab." She thought she was
   marrying an Israelite who was somebody, but she
   did not let the grief and trauma of her loss stop
   her. She was resilient. I encourage you to remain
   engaged in your assignment as Ruth did. Keep
   your heart open to new opportunities and do not
   get stuck thinking that God will work through
   only one way. Keep your eyes open for "suddenlies."
   As the Word says, "Unrelenting disappointment
   leaves you heartsick, but a sudden good break can
   turn life around" (Prov. 13:12, THE MESSAGE).

5. Have faith in God (Mark 11:22). Faith is confidence
   in God, not only that He exists, but that He is a
   rewarder of those who diligently seek Him (Heb.
   11:6). God is a good Father who gives good gifts to
   His children (Matt. 7:11). Our faith is built as we
   seek Him through His Word. Romans 10:17 says
   that faith comes by hearing, and hearing by the
   Word of God. In seeking Him, we find out who
   He is. We become acquainted with His character,
   that He is faithful and never leaves us alone (Heb.
   13:5). Our confidence will rise as we understand
   that God is with us wherever we go (Gen. 28:15;
   Deut. 31:8; Josh. 1:9).

We need to believe in ourselves as we are moved and empowered by God. Confidence is all about relying on God, having a courageous heart, and daring to press on despite fear. Some people get so comfortable with fear that even after deliverance they are still paralyzed in the same place. Fear has been a habit, an expectation. So they must activate courage in this instance by doing something. Once the spirit of fear has been cast out, you still have to do something. You still have to activate your faith by taking the leap, taking that action and moving forward. This is what we see in Ruth's decision to move with Naomi to Bethlehem.

Sometimes we do not even know that we have overcome something until we act. We do not know the extent of our strength and freedom. We do not know what we are made of because we are still held back by the idea that we are bound.

I challenge you now to look at your situation through the eyes of the Spirit and see where you need to make some moves. I challenge you to activate your faith right now and be ready to get moving with God at a moment's notice. Is there an opportunity waiting around for your yes? Is there a task that you need to check off your list, but you have been procrastinating? I challenge you to push yourself to say yes where you need to say yes and to get the things done that need to get done. Do not be the one to hold back your own breakthrough. You have what it takes. You are well equipped. You are the brightest one at the table. Do not doubt yourself. Do not doubt God. You are in the right place at the right time. You are not here by mistake. Take hold of the place God has you in and leverage what He put in your hand to be fruitful. It is all for His glory.

COME THROUGH, RUTH!

I love the phrase *come through*. It sometimes refers to when people are allowed to enter into greatness after a hard ordeal. Their time to shine has come and all those in the area know it. They have struggled and survived. They have been oppressed and downtrodden yet have finally broken through. This is the season for women to come through. God is empowering us to break through barriers and overcome obstacles set up to derail us from our God-given destiny. We are breaking through and our time to arise and shine is here. So come through!

PRAYER TO ACTIVATE GOD CONFIDENCE

Father, I declare that you are the God of my salvation and the confidence of all the ends of the earth and far-off seas (Ps. 65:5). I declare: It is better to trust in the Lord than to put confidence in man. It is better to trust in the Lord than to put confidence in princes (Ps. 118:8–9).

Lord, You are my confidence. You will keep my foot from being caught (Prov. 3:26). Lord, I find refuge in You, and in the fear of the Lord I find strong confidence (Prov. 14:26).

PRAYER TO BREAK BARRIERS

A breakthrough is a sudden, dramatic, and important discovery or development. I decree that this is my season of breakthrough. I decree that every limitation and barrier obstructing my destiny is broken. I will not be defined by my economic status. I will not be limited by my gender or race. I decree that every ceiling keeping me down is broken. I am a woman who will expand and break out on the left and the right. I will accomplish everything the Lord has designed for my life. I will rise up and stand up in the anointing. I speak to every mountain of fear and command you to be moved and cast into the sea. I will rise above prejudice and every preconceived opinion about my abilities as a woman. I break every generational curse of poverty and lack. I press on toward the high calling in Christ Jesus. I am a trailblazer. I will finish strong. I will come through!

Chapter 7

A WOMAN OF VIRTUE
AND EXCELLENCE

All the people of my town know that you are a virtuous
woman.

—RUTH 3:11, NKJV

RUTH IS THE only woman in the Bible called a virtuous woman,
and perhaps she was the inspiration for Proverbs 31, which her
great-great-grandson Solomon wrote. He would have learned
of her life as a child listening to his family's oral history. Ruth's
legacy of virtue is what has inspired this book. *Virtue* is the
Hebrew word *chayil*, which means "wealth, power, honor, virtuous, or strength." The word can also mean "army" or "force."[1]
It can refer to the ability to acquire wealth and riches. It is also
an attribute assigned to one who is upright and full of integrity. I believe God is highlighting and bringing revelation about
what it means to be a virtuous woman. I must admit in my
earlier years I heard this attribute taught exclusively for stay-
at-home moms who were the background to their husbands
foreground. "Behind every good man there is a good woman"—
the virtuous woman. Since I was divorced with a child by
the time I was twenty-five, I felt disqualified; this couldn't
be speaking of me. Maybe you are reading this book and feel
as if you're not qualified to be called virtuous. I want you to
know that virtue is a God-given force deposited in women to

prevail in any situation. If you have received Christ as your Lord and Savior, you are a candidate to operate in virtue.

THE SUPERNATURAL POWER OF VIRTUE

Through the life of Christ, who is in Ruth's family line, we learn that virtue is not only an attribute but also a supernatural force given to us by the power of the Holy Spirit. Evidence of this is found in Luke 8:43–48, the story of the woman with the issue of blood. Jesus had been ministering to large crowds all day and was on His way to perform another miracle—to raise a young girl from the dead. But a woman who had been bleeding for twelve years learned that Jesus was passing through her town. She pressed her way to Jesus, reached out, and touched the hem of His garment. In that instant Jesus turned and said, "Somebody hath touched me: for I perceive that virtue is gone out of me" (v. 46, KJV). The Greek word here for *virtue* is *dynamis*, which means "strength, power, or ability." *Dynamis* can mean "inherent power, power residing in a thing by virtue of its nature, or which a person or thing exerts and puts forth; power for performing miracles; moral power and excellence of soul; the power and influence which belong to riches and wealth; power and resources arising from numbers; or power consisting in or resting upon armies, forces, hosts."[2]

By extension, we can see that Ruth put out this same miraculous, supernatural force as she took on the role of securing the future of her family. Ruth's virtue was a miraculous, life-giving force to be reckoned with. Her virtue was like the power that rests upon an army. It was even said that Ruth was better to Naomi than seven sons! Seven is the number of completion and perfection. There is an anointing coming upon women to bring completion and satisfaction in their lives. The days of feeling empty and helpless are over. God is releasing an overcoming grace to prevail against every assignment of destruction and devastation.

> Then the women said to Naomi, "Blessed is the LORD who has not left you without a redeemer (grandson, as heir) today, and may his name become famous in Israel. May he also be to you one who restores life and sustains your old age; for your daughter-in-law, who loves you and is better to you than seven sons, has given birth to him."
>
> —RUTH 4:14–15

Ruth was empowered by the Holy Spirit to work hard, bring healing and joy to Naomi, and restore wealth and dignity to the name of her family. Modern-day Ruths will receive this same grace and empowerment to build, or in some cases rebuild, their lives. In following God and being aligned with His plan for her life, Ruth had all of heaven at her disposal. And as it was in the story of Elisha, there were more with her than against her. (See 2 Kings 6:16.) The virtuous power operating in Ruth enabled her to accomplish the work that needed to be done. Remember God is the same yesterday, today, and forever (Heb. 13:8). If He did for Ruth, who believed God under the old covenant, imagine what He can do for you with the new and better covenant. Let's take a look now at the virtuous nature of Ruth through the lens of Proverbs 31.

RUTH—A PROVERBS 31 WOMAN

> Who can find a virtuous woman? For her worth is far above rubies.
>
> —PROVERBS 31:10, MEV

Discussions on whether Proverbs 31 represents one woman or a composite of many women have gone back and forth since the time the Scripture passage was written. It may sound too good to be true, but as we think of mothers and wives who lead ministries or work outside their homes, it seems possible that Proverbs 31 is talking about you, me, your best friend, your aunt, or your mother. I also believe that as the first and only named virtuous woman in the Bible, Ruth has set the precedent.[3]

She is supportive (Prov. 31:10–12).

When the message of the virtuous woman is taught, we are normally pointed in the direction of a woman being supportive of her husband and her children. With Ruth, we find her supportiveness shown in her relationship with her mother-in-law. She was such a support to her mother-in-law that news of her support spread throughout the town like juicy gossip. Boaz said, "It has been fully reported to me, all that you have done for your mother-in-law since the death of your husband, and how you have left your father and your mother and the land of your birth, and have come to a people whom you did not know before" (Ruth 2:11, NKJV). Whether Ruth meant for people to know this about her or not, her kindness and support became the talk of the town. Modern-day Ruths will be known by this same kind of loyalty and support. Their virtuous reputation will precede them.

She takes initiative (Prov. 31:13–15).

> So Ruth the Moabitess said to Naomi, "Please let me go to the field, and glean heads of grain after him in whose sight I may find favor."
>
> —RUTH 2:2, NKJV

Taking a few days to sightsee in the new town she just arrived in was not on Ruth's to-do list. First things first for her was to get to work. As silent observers we know the devastating loss

Ruth has endured. Yet she was still seeking how she could contribute to the well-being of her family, recently reduced to only her and Naomi. By this simple request Ruth demonstrated that she was a self-starter, assertive, and solution-oriented. Ruth did not need anyone to tell her what to do next. She saw the needs in front of her and took initiative to meet them.

Many times we wait for things to be in place before we start a business or step into what we believe God has called us to do. Modern-day Ruths must believe that God is and that He is a rewarder of those who diligently seek Him (Heb. 11:6). Modern-day Ruths must begin right where they are. You may have to work for a temporary agency that specializes in the field of your desired business, learning the inner workings of the business. God may lead you to volunteer at a hospital, developing in you the capacity to serve. When you understand that destiny is fulfilled in steps that are ordered by God, complacency is no longer an option.

She is enterprising (Prov. 31:16).

The Bible says that God has given us the power to get wealth (Deut. 8:18). Ruth had an eye for how to work in a way that caused her to reach her provisionary goals quickly and efficiently. She took inventory of all the fields in her area and chose the one she thought might enable her to meet her goal for the day but also in which she could find favor to reach that goal more quickly and easily—a field where she would not only gather as much grain as she needed but also one in which she would be unhindered by molesters. A good businesswoman surveys all factors that may positively or negatively influence her goals. On her first day out Ruth found the field that would not only meet her immediate financial need but one that she could grow in and eventually own. I want to challenge you as a modern-day Ruth to develop a business mind. Instead of spending money frivolously on yourself, become a wise manager of your resources. Educate yourself so you are able to make wise financial decisions for your future. I believe God has given us power to get wealth.

Another thing that speaks to Ruth's business savvy is that when she came home to tell Naomi about her first day at work, she did not say, "Guess who I got to work for today?" She said, "The man's name with whom I worked today is Boaz" (Ruth 2:19, NKJV). Notice the phrase *with whom I worked.* Most people say, "…*for* whom I work" or "I work *for* so-and-so." Again demonstrating that she was of a different spirit, Ruth immediately positioned herself as a partner, not simply as an entry-level employee who punches the clock and is interested only in getting a check. She saw herself as a valuable contributor and aligned with the vision of the organization as one who would come alongside the owner to accomplish mutual goals. This is what you say when you work *with* someone.

She is responsible (Prov. 31:18).

Just as we discovered in the section above on initiative, Ruth proved herself responsible by taking the initiative to work to provide for both Naomi and herself. There was no man yet set as provider over the two women. Naomi was an older woman who was not able to work. So without giving it much thought, Ruth took on the role as provider, and she did so with excellence and expedience, so much so that the whole town took notice.

In another example we see that when she received instruction from Naomi on how to approach Boaz with the idea of redeeming her family's estate, she also took ownership of the outcome.

And she said to her, "All that you say to me I will do." So
she went down to the threshing floor and did according to
all that her mother-in-law instructed her.
—RUTH 3:5–6, NKJV

We are responsible for what we say and what we do. When
we do what we say we will do, we take ownership of our actions.
We are saying that we take responsibility for what happens
next. Responsibility is about being accountable to something
or someone. Responsible people are trustworthy and reliable.
Ruth was someone Naomi could count on.

She is humanitarian (Prov. 31:20).

Although Ruth and Naomi were in immediate need at the
beginning of the Book of Ruth, we know the generations of
good they produced for their offspring. Ruth set the tone for
prosperity and changed the economic outlook for her whole
family. Her outreach efforts started first with her mother-in-
law. Realizing Naomi could not work but still needed provision, Ruth stepped in to make sure she had all she needed.

One of the most outstanding qualities of modern-day Ruths
will be their care for the poor. I believe the Lord causes a generation who have hearts to serve to arise. I pray that the Lord
will train your eye to see those who are in need. I pray that
you will extend your hand in love to help them. I want to challenge you to volunteer to mentor a young woman. Start at
your church serving a widow. Many of the seniors in my local
church are on fixed income, and I find myself giving them a
"Pentecostal handshake," putting some cash in their hands.

As women get older, their risk of living in extreme poverty
increases. In the United States almost twice as many women
as men over the age of sixty-five live in poverty.[4] Through their
gifts, modern-day Ruths are well positioned to change poverty

statistics for women and children around the globe. The Ruth anointing is one that will work to stabilize women's economic forecasts through entrepreneurship, nonprofit organizations, advocacy, and education.

She is a woman of excellence (Prov. 31:21–25).

Ruth was a woman of excellence. In the Amplified version of the Bible, Ruth 3:11 reads, "All my people in the city know that you are a woman of excellence." Instead of the word *virtue*, as it says in other translations, Boaz calls her "a woman of excellence." *Excellence* can be defined as "extremely high quality," and is associated with words such as *distinction, greatness, perfection*, and *superiority*.[5] Though excellence is connected to perfection, I believe that excellence is of God while the desire for perfection in many cases is from the enemy. Excellence connects with a humble confidence. Excellence is an attitude. Excellence isn't tangible but is something noticeable. I believe excellence is a heart issue. Ruth believed in her heart, confessed with her mouth, and put action to her faith, and she found favor and promotion. Modern-day Ruths will behave in a spirit of excellence that speaks faith in the midst of adversity and looks for the silver lining in the cloud and the light at the end of the tunnel. There is a high quality associated with excellence. Seeking perfection in some sense is approval- and fear-based and is manifested by those who have not been healed from a spirit of rejection. True excellence is based on humility, faith in God, and His supernatural grace that empowers you to go beyond the average expectation.

She is careful with her words (Prov. 31:26).

Ruth was a woman of honor who had tremendous respect and preference toward her elders and those in authority over her. Yet she had a special gift for what many in the business world call managing up. She first demonstrated this in chapter 1 of the Book of Ruth, where she told Naomi, "Do not urge me to leave you or to turn back from following you; for where you go, I will go" (Ruth 1:16). She was not being disrespectful, but she was expressing what she felt as the best way forward for what she knew God had in her and Naomi's future. She also saw the state Naomi was in, and Naomi's bitterness could have sabotaged Ruth's hopefulness for what God had for her if Ruth let it. But she did not. Her statement was her establishment of a boundary and her management of the word she held in her heart regarding her next season.

The few other times that we "hear" Ruth speak, it is in this same direct and respectful tone. When she spoke to Boaz, she said, "I am Ruth your maid. Spread the hem of your garment over me, for you are a close relative and redeemer" (Ruth 3:9). Ruth let him know specifically what she needed and how he could help her accomplish the redemption of her family's estate. She used the authority God gave her over her destiny—for who on the outside looking in would know Ruth's destiny better than Ruth? Who knows what God has spoken to you better than you? It is critical that Ruths learn how to manage the human resources that God brings them in contact with.

Ruth spoke with confidence in the direction she knew God was leading her in, and she used both her words and actions to guide and position those around her to join in with what God wanted to do.

"She opens her mouth with wisdom, and on her tongue is the law of kindness" (Prov. 31:26, NKJV). The modern-day Ruth will have supernatural wisdom. She will use her words graciously. She will not speak foolishly or with evil intent.

She is strong (Prov. 31:27–29).

Ruth was physically strong as well as spiritually and emo-tionally strong. She did not let her circumstances keep her from doing what she knew she needed to do to get herself out of the low place she was in. She did not allow herself to be defined by her circumstances. Instead she got to work. Field work is not easy. She had to stoop and bend all day long as the weight of the grain grew heavier by the minute as she filled her bag. But she worked with such determination and efficiency that she caught the attention of those around her.

Modern-day Ruths must take care of their health. The Proverb 31 woman strengthened her arms. I believe during times of restoration and recovery, we can forget about our natural health, but we must strengthen ourselves to fulfill our destinies.

She is godly (Prov. 31:30).

Following Ruth's declaration in Ruth 1:16—"...and your God, my God"—every action she made was made to honor her new God and His people. Modern-day Ruths will have strong faith in God. They will have reverent submission to the Lord. I believe Ruth served Naomi fervently because she did everything as unto the Lord. Modern-day Ruths will have hearts to please the Lord with their actions. Everything they do will be to impress God, not people. Modern-day Ruths will be known for their reverence and obedience to the ways of God. This is what makes them exceptional and praiseworthy. The woman who fears the Lord is one of impeccable character; she is trustworthy and industrious and makes great financial decisions. She is a woman prepared for the future.

She is diligent (Prov. 31:13, 27).

One of the characteristics of the virtuous woman is that she is willing to get to work to accomplish what needs to be done; she is not idle (Prov. 31:13, 27). Ruth embodied these characteristics, and as a result she was indeed rewarded with wealth and abundant supply for all she needed. Proverbs 12:24 says, "The hand of the diligent will rule, but the negligent and lazy will be put to forced labor." Then Proverbs 13:4 says, "The soul (appetite) of the lazy person craves and gets nothing [for lethargy overcomes ambition], but the soul (appetite) of the diligent [who works willingly] is rich and abundantly supplied."

What if Ruth had given in to her grief? What if, when she got to Bethlehem, she stayed home with Naomi? What if she allowed depression to lead to laziness and procrastination? Sometimes when we nurse our trauma and broken places too long and do not get ministry and deliverance, we end up manifesting things that sabotage our success. Diligence brings reward, favor, blessing, and wealth into our lives: "the hand of the diligent makes him rich" (Prov. 10:4). Diligence is the precious possession of a wise person; a diligent woman is one who "recognizes opportunities and seizes them" (Prov. 12:27). You cannot just see something out in the distance that may be possible. You have to be willing to get up and go see about it.

The enemy of diligence is slothfulness. Slothfulness is connected to many vices and negative consequences:

+ Lack—"The soul of the sluggard craves and gets nothing, while the soul of the diligent is richly supplied" (Prov. 13:4, ESV). "The sluggard will not plow because of the cold; therefore he will beg during harvest and have nothing" (Prov. 20:4, MEV).

+ Laziness—"The desire of the slothful kills him, for his hands refuse to labor" (Prov. 21:25, MEV).

- Hardship—"The way of the slothful man is as a hedge of thorns, but the way of the righteous is made plain" (Prov. 15:19, MEV).

- Spirit of slumber and withdrawal from life—"How long will you sleep, O sluggard? When will you arise out of your sleep?" (Prov. 6:9, MEV). "Slothfulness casts into a deep sleep, and an idle soul will suffer hunger" (Prov. 19:15, MEV).

- Waste, ruin, and poverty—"He also that is slothful in his work is brother to him that is a great waster" (Prov. 18:9, KJV). "I went by the field of the slothful, and by the vineyard of the man void of understanding; and it was all grown over with thorns, and nettles covered its surface, and the stone wall was broken down. Then I saw, and considered it; I looked on it and received instruction: yet a little sleep, a little slumber, a little folding of the hands to sleep, so your poverty will come like a stalker, and your need as an armed man" (Prov. 24:30–34, MEV).

- Wickedness—"But his master answered him, 'You wicked and slothful servant! You knew that I reap where I have not sown and gather where I scattered no seed?'" (Matt. 25:26, ESV).

Diligence means "steady, earnest, and energetic effort; persevering application."[6] Those who put in the effort and are faithful and patient inherit the promises of God. Hebrews 6:11–12 says, "We desire that every one of you show the same diligence for the full assurance of hope to the end, so that you may not be lazy, but imitators of those who through faith and patience inherit the promises" (MEV).

Women with the Ruth anointing are diligent, faithful, patient, and hardworking, looking to the promises of God set before them. No matter what is happening in their lives, they do not shut down; they get to work. They do not give in to a lazy and slothful spirit. They know what to do to keep themselves full of hope and assurance. If you find that you have been edging toward inaction and slothfulness, here are some things you can to do recharge yourself:

+ Find a place to serve. Look around your God zone. Volunteer. Sometimes you have to be put in a position to use your gifts. Give. Be generous. Naomi and Ruth were in the same position, but Ruth chose to move beyond. Take the focus off yourself.

+ Do not procrastinate. If this is your issue, find an accountability partner. Move yourself from only making declarations to making demonstrations concerning what the Lord is doing in your life. Do not put off for tomorrow what you can do today (Prov. 6:4, NLT).

+ Start small and take advantage of what is available. When you are lofty and high-minded, you can miss the things God has for you. Humble yourself, and think outside the box. God's ways are not our ways. Expand your expectation of what God wants to do in your life.

Diligence brings blessing, favor, promotion, wealth, and increase. Diligence stretches the limits of your faithfulness to God. When God sees your diligence in the small things, He will make you ruler of much, just as He did for Ruth.

From Gleaner to Owner of the Field

Gleaning was a form of charity for the disadvantaged in ancient Israel. God made special provision in the Law for the poor, foreigners, widows, and orphans to walk behind the harvesters and pick up the grain the farmers dropped and purposely left behind (Lev. 19:9–10; 23:22; Deut. 24:19). The law forbade farmers from reaping the corners of their grain fields or picking up any grain they dropped. They were to leave it for people who were in situations similar to that of Ruth and Naomi.[7] Even though she was new in town, Ruth somehow observed that this was something she could do instead of begging or prostitution. But she did not remain a gleaner very long. Promotion came quickly. I believe that this will also be the case for modern-day Ruths. It will not be long that you will work with all diligence before breakthrough, favor, and promotion comes. In order to move from being an employee to an owner, a follower to a leader, Ruths need to look out for:

+ Divine shifts—Be ready to move with the Spirit of God. Be ready to say to the Lord, "Where You go, I will go."

+ Transitions—Do not be afraid of change and sudden movements of the Holy Spirit. Remain flexible and keep your eyes on God. Seasons change, but each one serves a purpose in preparing you for your destiny. In transition is where God perfects your character so you can sustain the seasons of abundance and plenty.

+ Fear of moving from obscurity to prominence—In the last chapter we discussed competence versus confidence. In developing the Ruth anointing, some women will need to release their fear of being seen and known. Ruth took an enormous risk emigrating from the idolatrous nation of Moab to the God-fearing, chosen nation of Israel. Among the Jewish people, she stood out with her Moabite attire, accent, and customs. She could not hide. Her presence and contributions were immediately made known throughout the town. The Ruth anointing will call you out of obscurity. You will not be able to hide behind a false sense of humility and insecurity. Ruths are full of God confidence and are ready to bear the responsibility of being visible for God's glory to be seen through them.

+ Opportunities to be faithful where you are—We do not know where God will place us. Ruth did not have a list of what she wanted God to do for her in her new town. She did not go up to the leaders of the town and demand a place on the executive team. She looked at where she was and what she could do and took hold of the opportunities around her. It was not Ruth's ambition that brought her success; it was her faithfulness and diligence. Matthew 25:23 says, "Well done, good and faithful servant. You have been faithful and trustworthy over a little, I will put you in charge of many things; share in the joy of your master."

+ Patience—Promotion comes from God. Do not rush. Patience was part of Ruth's virtue. She had no idea what awaited her, yet she did not fret. She had the resolve to deal with what she faced today and let tomorrow take care of itself (Matt. 6:34).

She embodied the message of Proverbs 31:25: "She is clothed with strength and dignity, and she laughs without fear of the future" (NLT). Patience also gave her strength to endure the tough season. She did not grow weary in doing well, and in due season she reaped a bountiful harvest (Gal. 6:9). All that she had lost was returned to her one hundredfold.

God wants to give you the capacity to see beyond where you are. Your picture must be bigger than what you see right now. God says, "I will do a new thing. Now it shall spring forth; shall you not know it?" (Isa. 43:19, NKJV). This scripture indicates that God is working, but many times we cannot perceive His masterful mighty hand. We must learn how to live in the present moment while always embracing the future. New things will stretch us, causing us to "be made or be capable of being made longer or wider without tearing or breaking."[8]

Are you willing to be stretched? Remember, if you are settling for the status quo, you are already disqualified. Stretching involves change. Stretching sets you apart. Stretching opens the door to a life of significance. Stretching causes you to grow, and real growth stops when you lose the tension between where you are and where you want to be. Ruth was willing to be stretched. She was not afraid of trying new things.

Familiar things resist the new thing. Comfort is the enemy of the new thing. When was the last time you were stretched? When was the last time you were bold enough to step out of your comfort zone to embrace a new position or assignment? This is what it takes to go from where you are to where you know God wants and needs you to be. Gleaning was not all God had for Ruth. If she was not willing to follow God wherever He led, saying, "Yes, God, I will go. I will do as You have commanded," she would not have received her promise. She would not have been a mother in the line of Christ. That was her destiny.

From idolater to worshipper of the one true God, Ruth is our model for what blessings come when we are willing to say yes to the new thing. We can start right where we are and with what we have in our hand. The supernatural virtue in the Ruth anointing is a miraculous multiplying agent that causes faithfulness and diligence to bring unimaginable promotion and increase to all who apply it.

PRAYER FOR DILIGENCE AND FOR BREAKING A SLOTHFUL SPIRIT

The hand of the diligent shall bear rule: but the slothful shall be under tribute.

—PROVERBS 12:24, KJV

I decree that I am a woman who exercises diligence in every area of my life. I am creative and resourceful. I decree that everything my hands touch prospers. I am enterprising. I break every slothful, lazy spirit from my life. I will not lie around and think about what I want to do, but I will take action to fulfill my dreams. I decree that my hands are blessed. I have the hand of the diligent, and I will create my world and rule it. I will use my brain, talents, and gifts to empower others. I will break the spirit of procrastination off my life. I will not leave things undone. I will be productive in every area of my life. I am a woman who takes the initiative, and I follow through. I will not make excuses. I will look for favor and not wait for favor to find me.

Chapter 8

THE POWER OF REDEMPTION
AND RESTORATION

You are witnesses this day that I have bought everything
that was Elimelech's and everything that was Chilion's and
Mahlon's from the hand of Naomi. I have also acquired
Ruth the Moabitess, the widow of Mahlon, to be my wife
to restore the name of the deceased to his inheritance, so
that the name of the deceased will not be cut off from his
brothers or from the gate of his birthplace. You are witnesses today.

—RUTH 4:9–10

At the core of the story of Ruth is the loving and redemptive heart of God. Ruths are different. They are diverse. They
are not of the same household or the right family. They are
not always from the affluent part of town, and their people
may be marginalized. But what cannot be denied is the ever-
lasting love and favor of God upon the lives of those with the
Ruth anointing. When Ruths get ahold of this, their resolve
to follow Him to a place of total redemption, restoration, and
destiny is unshakeable. Upon learning of a loving God who
sees them as He sees His own chosen people, they will find
their places and take up the mantle of pursuing Him and His
purposes without wavering.

Ruth was ready to follow Naomi wherever her path wound

up. She was ready to do whatever she needed to do to restore the inheritance due to Naomi's family name. Together they used the provisions God had in place to reinstate a redemptive agency so powerful that it would ultimately extend to you and me, whom the Bible calls Gentiles, and those whom without the redemption of Jesus Christ would not be able to lay claim to the benefits and blessings of being grafted into the line of Christ. Ruth set a precedent for all people everywhere—every nation, kindred, tongue, and people—to receive the blessings that were once exclusive to the Jewish people, the sons and daughters of Abraham, Jacob, and Isaac. But through Ruth's faith and virtue we now walk in a whole new destiny.

THE LEVIRATE LAW—A LAW OF REDEMPTION

Ruth was ready and willing, faithful and hardworking, but she did not know Jewish custom. Enter Naomi. As I have said, Naomi was an older and respected woman in her town. She was well versed in her culture and all the provisions God made in the Law of Moses for her and her people to live under the blessing and protection of God's covenant with them. When Naomi realized that Ruth had been granted favor in the fields of a close relative, she got a sense of the Lord's favor returning to her life. She knew the time had come for her to teach a special redemptive provision to her daughter-in-law. This provision is called the levirate law or the law of the levirate marriage, from the Hebrew word for brother. The law required a man to marry his brother's childless widow so that the brother's "name will not be blotted out of Israel" (Deut. 25:6). If no brother was available, another male relative might be asked to fulfill the law, but the widow had to let him know he was acceptable as her goel, her kinsman-redeemer and provider. Naomi told Ruth exactly how to let Boaz know he was acceptable as Ruth's kinsman-redeemer. Ruth carefully listened to Naomi's words and carried them out to the letter.[1]

In my own experience in church and listening to sermon after sermon on the romance and redemption story in the Book of Ruth, I heard time and time again how Ruth's actions of laying at Boaz's feet on the floor of the threshing floor was quite risqué. Maybe you learned the same thing. But upon further study I learned that what Ruth did was directed and approved by a respected older woman and was a custom of the time for a woman seeking to have her estate redeemed by a close relative after the death of her husband. It is described in Deuteronomy 25:5–10.

> If brothers are living together and one of them dies without a son, the widow of the deceased shall not be married outside the family to a stranger. Her husband's brother shall be intimate with her after taking her as his wife and perform the duty of a husband's brother to her. It shall be that her firstborn [son] will be given the name of the dead brother, so that his name will not be blotted out of Israel. But if the man does not want to marry his brother's [widowed] wife, then she shall go up to the gate [of the city, where court is held] to the elders, and say, "My brother-in-law refuses to continue his brother's name in Israel; he is not willing to perform the duty of a husband's brother." Then the elders of his city will summon him and speak to him. And if he stands firm and says, "I do not want to marry her," then his brother's widow shall approach him in the presence of the elders, and pull his sandal off his foot and spit in his face; and she shall answer and say, "So it is done to that man who does not build up his brother's household." In Israel his [family] name shall be, "The house of him whose sandal was removed."

Knowing this allowance in the Law, Naomi instructed, "Now Boaz, with whose maids you were [working], is he not our relative? See now, he is winnowing barley at the threshing floor tonight. So wash and anoint yourself [with olive oil], then put on your [best] clothes, and go down to the threshing floor; but stay out of the man's sight until he has finished eating and drinking. When he lies down, notice the place where he is lying, and go and uncover his feet and lie down. Then he will tell you what to do" (Ruth 3:2–4). If Boaz was willing, the next step in this custom was for him to cover her with his blanket. This would symbolize that he was up to the responsibility of being a covering for Ruth both in marriage and as a redeemer for her household.

I have heard some preachers frame this exchange as the stereotypical female maneuvering and manipulation, that Ruth and Naomi set out on a matchmaking plot to hook a man. Yet they failed to dive in deep to Jewish law and custom. There was no inappropriate behavior here on Ruth's part. There was no fleshly scheme to pounce upon an unsuspecting eligible bachelor. As we unpacked in the last chapter, Ruth was a woman of virtue, honor, and excellence. She would have been stripped of these attributes if she violated the social norms. The women were operating within the provisions God made to help save families from the desolation that can come when the main breadwinner dies.

So as Ruth set out to do all Naomi asked her to do, I imagine she kept this in the front of her mind as she was resolute but maybe a little nervous. How well did she know Boaz? Would he accept her? Was Naomi right? At the threshing floor Ruth saw Boaz lying down just as Naomi had said. She went in quietly, uncovered his feet, and lay down. This was a symbol of her desire to be redeemed by Boaz. Though he was startled at first, Boaz was aware of his position and responsibility at that point. I would even dare to say that he may have thought of Ruth and Naomi's plight upon hearing of their return to the town. His kindness to her upon their first meeting seems premeditated in some aspects. He had already worked out in his mind how he might make life easier for her and her mother-in-law. And now the fullness of his role as redeemer became apparent. He was willing and ready.

> So he said, "Who are you?" And she answered, "I am Ruth your maid. Spread the hem of your garment over me, for you are a close relative and redeemer." Then he said, "May you be blessed by the LORD, my daughter. You have made your last kindness better than the first; for you have not gone after young men, whether poor or rich. Now, my daughter, do not be afraid. I will do for you whatever you ask, since all my people in the city know that you are a woman of excellence. It is true that I am your close relative and redeemer; however, there is a relative closer [to you] than I. Spend the night [here], and in the morning if he will redeem you, fine; let him do it. But if he does not wish to redeem you, then, as the LORD lives, I will redeem you. Lie down until the morning."
>
> —RUTH 3:9–13

"I will redeem you"—the comfort, security, love, and protection in these words is the same message the Father speaks to Ruths today. In Hebrew this concept translates as to "do the part of next of kin, act as kinsman-redeemer, avenge, revenge, ransom."[2] Looking at those last three words, it almost seems as if the redeemer comes to right some wrongs or injustices that occurred, as indeed they did. The barriers Ruth faced in her day and the barriers we face now as modern-day Ruths are wrongs committed by society, tradition, religion, and the hearts of sinful men. Our Redeemer comes to avenge us and to ransom us from the fate of this unjust world. And like our divine Redeemer did, Boaz swooped in and took up Ruth's cause without hesitation. He lifted the responsibility of provider off her shoulders. He would take it from there. All she needed to do was to go home and wait. It turned out that the other kinsman, who was a closer relative to Elimelech, did not want to redeem her, which left Boaz able to fulfill the promise he made to her on the threshing floor.

BEFORE YOU ENTER THE THRESHING FLOOR

The threshing floor is an important scene in the story of Ruth. It is both a physical and spiritual place where good and evil are sorted. But before Ruth could go to the threshing floor, she needed to properly prepare. Naomi led her through the steps: "So wash and anoint yourself [with olive oil], then put on your [best] clothes, and go down to the threshing floor" (Ruth 3:3).

Much like apostle Paul said in Philippians 3:13–14, Naomi encouraged Ruth to take deliberate steps to forget all they had been through, to the point of putting on her best outfit and reaching out to the things that lay ahead. It was morning for Ruth (Ps. 30:5). Joy was returning to the women's lives. What was once sad and bitter was being exchanged for what would bring them joy and sweetness.

Let's take a closer look at what each step did to help Ruth prepare both physically and spiritually.

Wash yourself.

Ruth had been working hard and probably had not taken time to think of herself and how she appeared. Naomi told her that it was time for some self-care. We have talked about how as women we tend to consider ourselves last, especially in the midst of a crisis such as the one Naomi and Ruth had been facing. But here we find Naomi calling Ruth to look beyond their immediate circumstances, to see that it was time to transition. While she needed to physically wash, it was also a symbol. She was to wash off the past and be ready for her next season. Ruth prepared herself to be in close proximity to her redeemer.

Speaking of Jesus, the Bible says, "…so that He might sanctify the church, having cleansed her by the washing of water with the word [of God], so that [in turn] He might present the church to Himself in glorious splendor, without spot or wrinkle or any such thing; but that she would be holy [set apart for God] and blameless" (Eph. 5:26–27). Washing in this sense symbolizes sanctification. By washing in the water of the Word, modern-day Ruths prepare themselves to be in close proximity to their Redeemer.

Anoint yourself.

Throughout the Bible anointing oil is referred to as a means of setting something or someone apart for holy use. (See Leviticus 8:30; Numbers 4:16.) It is also a symbol of the Holy Spirit. (See the parable of the ten virgins in Matthew 25:1–13.) Just as Ruth needed the anointing of the Holy Spirit to properly prepare for the humility and vulnerability required to ask for a redeemer, modern-day Ruths need the empowering of the Spirit to perform the right task at the right time to secure the promises of God for their lives. Pride, fleshly desires, and selfishness will sabotage the purity of the blessing of God.

Though Ruth was well within her right to lay at Boaz's feet at night as he slept, lust of the flesh could have had its way in either of them and we would be reading an entirely different story. Just as with Ruth, there are some spiritually volatile circumstances modern-day Ruths will have to navigate through. They will need the anointing that breaks the yoke of the flesh in order to stay focused and pure.

Put on your best clothes.

Until this moment Ruth had been wearing the customary clothing of a widow. She was a woman in mourning, and she could not take the heaviness of her past, the loss of a husband, and all their dreams of a life together into the future with a new husband. She had to shed her widow's garment and put on something new that symbolized newness and a revived hope for her future.

Changing clothes in Scripture represents putting off the old life and putting on the new. For the modern-day Ruth there must be a deliberate action of letting go of the past. It is time to take off the old and put on the new.

THE THRESHING FLOOR

In the threshing floor scene Ruth symbolizes the believer, a Gentile, an outsider like me and maybe you too. Boaz is a representation of Christ, the Redeemer. Her request was made on the threshing floor among the grain and the chaff, giving us a beautiful image of man's need for salvation, God's role as Redeemer, and the way He separates us from the things that keep us from transitioning from where we are to where He wants us to be.

Threshing is the agricultural process of separating the wheat from the tares and straw by beating the stalks with a rod. It was done on a flat, level floor called the threshing floor. The Hebrew word is *duwsh*, meaning "to trample or thresh: break, tear, thresh, tread out."[3] Thinking of this as a separation of spirit from flesh, it sounds painful. But this separation must take place before we enter a new covenant with God. Just as Ruth's example demonstrates, we go from old marriage to new marriage, old life to new life, and past to future.

Through the Holy Spirit and your connection with covenant friends, you will discover the things you cannot carry into your new season. They are things you simply will no longer need. Whatever defined you in the old season, God will begin to remove it. Anything you trusted in—old labels, old mantle, and old mind-sets—will be trampled out. The threshing floor was Ruth's final place of surrender and uncompromising obedience, her proving and testing ground. Passing this test of submitting to the will of God for her life, she was able to eat the good of the land (Isa. 1:19).

"Spread the hem of your garment over me"

> I am Ruth your maid. Spread the hem of your garment over me, for you are a close relative and redeemer.
>
> —RUTH 3:9

As we discovered above, Ruth's request is honorable and does not constitute anything illicit or distasteful, but her request for Boaz to lay his garment over her is part of an ancient custom that carries significance for us today. The Hebrew word for hem ("corner" in the New International Version) literally means "wing," and is a "metaphor...used in [Ezekiel] 16:8 for the commitment of marriage. This symbolic language further creates a wordplay with Boaz's statement in [Ruth] 2:12 where he asserts that Ruth has found security under the 'wings' of the God of Israel. In essence, her request was to find further security under the wings of Boaz."[4] She was asking him to be her covering, protector, provider, and husband.

Ezekiel 16:8 says, "'Then I passed by you [again] and looked on you; behold, you were maturing and at the time for love, and I spread My skirt over you and covered your nakedness. Yes, I swore [an oath] to you and entered into a covenant with you,' says the Lord GOD, 'and you became Mine.'" Many women have felt uncovered, but on the threshing floor God will cover you, protect you, and secure your future. Boaz gave Ruth directions on the threshing floor. We find direction for our paths in the same place in the Spirit with God. He will straighten out the paths of His devoted servants.

After Boaz told her what he would do on her behalf before the town elders, Ruth left the threshing floor with a promise and grain that represented a foretaste of the life to come. Modern-day Ruths are women who will bow at the feet of Jesus, women who are dependent on His presence to cover them. They will believe in the power of His promise to deliver them. Malachi 4:2 says, "The Sun of Righteousness shall arise with healing in His wings" (NKJV). The word translated as "wings" is the same word translated as "hem" in Ruth 3:9. Jesus is the Sun of Righteousness, and He enables us to be freed from the weight and burden of the pain of the past as we bow at His feet and are covered by His healing wings.

At the feet of the redeemer

Ruth had to wait at Boaz's feet until daylight. The Bible says that weeping endures for a night, but joy comes in the morning (Ps. 30:5). Ruth had to endure the night and the darkness with patience. She had to wait for the promise to be fulfilled. There are many times we forfeit the promise in the night. Night represents times of bewilderment, blindness, and lack of comprehension of the will of God. This causes us to be impatient and many times to make irrational decisions. Modern

Ruths will learn how to trust in the Lord with their whole hearts, leaning not on their own understanding and acknowledging the Lord, and He will direct their paths (Prov. 3:5–6).

Let's examine the position in which Ruth waited—at Boaz's feet. In Luke 10:38–42 we find the story of another devoted follower of God, Mary, the sister of Martha and Lazarus. With so many other things to do, Mary did not give up one minute of her time at the feet of her Redeemer. The Bible says that she "seated herself at the Lord's feet and was continually listening to His teaching" (v. 39).

At the feet of the Redeemer is where we receive instruction on how to get to the next level. If we get impatient or distracted with the many things that need to get done, we can miss out on what the next right move is. I would dare to say that Mary was a type of Ruth in that she had a peace about doing the right thing in the right moment and was unmoved by the choices or judgments of others. Both women had a resolve that gave them an edge when it came time to level up. Though Jesus said it of Mary, I would like to believe He would say it about Ruth: that she had "chosen the good part [that which is to her advantage], which will not be taken away from her" (v. 42).

Where unwavering trust is built

The threshing floor is where we learn to trust God with all of our hearts. It is a place of intimacy. The very act of waiting there at Boaz's feet was an act of trust. We must cease from our labors and lay at the feet of our Redeemer. The Hebrew word translated "trust" in Ruth 2:12 is *chacah*, which means "to flee for protection; have hope; make refuge;."[5] It is the picture from Psalm 57:1 of David nestling under God's wings for refuge in the manner a defenseless baby bird hides under its parent's feathers. Boaz recognized Ruth's actions as trusting in the God of Israel for safety and refuge. We must stand still and know that we will see the salvation of the Lord (Exod. 14:13).

When Ruth lay at Boaz's feet and asked him to spread his garment over her, it was an honorable request to enter into the covenant of marriage. There is power in asking God for what you want. My grandmother taught that a closed mouth never got fed. The threshing floor is a place of prayer before the throne of God. There are days to make bold, out-of-the-box requests to your Redeemer. Lean into the timing of the Holy Spirit, and make those days count.

As your trust in God to provide and protect increases, you will release the details to Him. You do not have to have it all figured out. He already does. All you need to worry about is exercising the confidence to obey Him.

In due season, as you work hard and sacrifice, you will reap a reward, just as Ruth did. When the appointed time comes, God will elevate you to the position He has always had in His plans. The threshing floor is your place of intimacy and refinement, preparing you to handle all He will bring across your path.

FROM BARREN TO BLESSED

The blessing of redemption is that it is not partial when God does it. Everything that the enemy has stolen is restored to you sevenfold (Prov. 6:31), the number seven representing perfection. Nothing will be missing.

From Ruth chapter 1 we learned that Naomi lost her husband and two sons and was past childbearing age, and Ruth had been widowed without having had children. But through the process of redemption, Ruth conceived a son. His birth signified the restoration of Naomi's family line. Even the townspeople recognized what God had done:

> Then the women said to Naomi, "Blessed is the LORD who
> has not left you without a redeemer (grandson, as heir)
> today, and may his name become famous in Israel. May he
> also be to you one who restores life and sustains your old
> age; for your daughter-in-law, who loves you and is better
> to you than seven sons, has given birth to him....A son
> (grandson) has been born to Naomi."
>
> —RUTH 4:14–15, 17

The judgment of God had been lifted from Naomi's life.
She could once again live out the fullness of her name, which
means "my delight," or "pleasant."[6] No more being called
Mara. The lines had been drawn for these women, and they
fell in pleasant places; they now had a beautiful and blessed
heritage (Ps. 16:5–6).

TO A THOUSAND GENERATIONS

With its perfect, happily-ever-after ending, people often
describe the Book of Ruth as a love story. It certainly contains
those elements, but it is much more than that. It shows God's
desire to redeem all the peoples of the earth. From the time
of Abraham, God blessed and directed the lives of the people
of Israel through His exclusive covenant. But there were
always exceptions such as Ruth, the Moabite, the foreigner,
the Gentile, the idolater. Ruth's redemption story is an early
indicator that God did not want to save only Israel, but He
also wanted to save the world. And even more than that, He
wanted the entire world—every nation, kindred, tongue, and
people—to be included in His family line.

The legacy of Christ is unique and perfectly imperfect, by
the grace of God. God purposely orchestrated this to show

that all are welcome—different races, ethnicities, religious backgrounds, socioeconomic classes, and education levels.

Ruth the Moabite became a mother in the line of Christ Himself, and she was the only woman in the Bible to be specifically named a virtuous woman. She was pulled up from a place of defeat and opposition to the people of God to becoming an example for all people who feel marginalized. Through her all those who had once been far off are now drawn in close to the heart of the Father. She was instrumental in breaking down the dividing wall that keeps the people of God from coming together. Looking back at all the barriers Ruth broke through, there is not one person who should be excluded from God's plan of redemption. It is not God's will that any should perish (2 Pet. 3:9).

Ruth's act of going to the threshing floor was an act of total obedience, believing that God would deliver her. Ruth had already made her declaration of faith back in Moab. Ruth understood she was taking a risk that could damage her reputation, but even as Jesus made Himself of no reputation, she too had made a decision to faithfully follow the leading of God and do what Naomi instructed under the grace of God.

Modern-day Ruths must walk the path of faith, going against the grain of the status quo. We must blaze new trails under the leadership of the Holy Ghost. God is causing those who endure the threshing floor process to experience complete recovery, restoration, and resurrection power to receive their inheritance in the Lord!

Woman of God, it is time to live your dream! It is time to do what God determined for you before you were in your mother's womb. I believe that there are people and places waiting for you to arise and embrace your destiny. Walking into your destiny, even if you are just starting out or if you are completely starting over, will require a different spirit. We must understand that the end of a thing is always better than the beginning (Eccles. 7:8). God will give you the power to overcome any obstacle that hinders your destiny. As we make decisions to follow the Lord with our whole hearts, trusting His heart and plan for our lives even when we do not understand the painful and sometimes tragic events we may encounter on the road to destiny, these are the days that will lead us to fulfill our ultimate purpose in life. You were never designed by God to live a mundane, mediocre life. Great men and women were born for the time they are needed most! God is releasing courage and clarity to align with His purpose for your life. As you endure the process, the Lord is unlocking greatness inside you. It is not your responsibility to figure out the process; it is your responsibility to say yes! If you are willing and obedient, you will eat the good of the land. The powerful thing about this statement is that God works in you to both to will and do His good pleasure (Phil. 2:13). The odds stacked against you do not matter. Do not allow racism, sexism, or classism to defeat or define you. The Lord is releasing tenacity and determination in your heart to live out your destiny! You are a world changer!

Prayer That Activates
the Voice of Destiny

Lord, I believe Your Word that the end of a thing is better than the beginning. Thank You, Lord, for the great things You have in store for me. I decree that the race is not given to the swift or strong but to the one that endures to the end (Eccles. 9:11). I submit my will to Your will. I decree that I am an overcomer. I am a barrier breaker. Thank You, Lord, that You redeemed my life from destruction. I break every limitation in my mind. I take off every garment designed to keep me in a place of defeat. I will arise from fear and inaction and live the life God destined me to live. I am a world changer. I will set the course of my entire family. Like Ruth I am a bloodline restorer. I make life decisions that will activate a chain of blessing for the generations to come. I trust You, Lord, with my process. I lay my life at Your feet! Just like Jesus I trust You for resurrection. I say, "Not my will but Your will be done in my life."

Father, I thank You for redeeming the times and restoring the years in my life. I embrace my divine purpose. I will not allow hurt, pain, or loss to keep me in a place of stagnation. Lord, give me fresh momentum in my life. I choose to listen to the voice of destiny. I will not listen to the voice of defeat. I will not listen to the voice of fear or failure. I am a woman of faith, virtue, and destiny.

NOTES

Introduction
Your Destiny Is Calling

1. Matthew Henry, *Matthew Henry Commentary on the Whole Bible (Concise)*, Bible Study Tools, accessed August 11, 2017, http://www.biblestudytools.com/commentaries/matthew-henry-concise/ruth/1.html.

2. *Oxford English Dictionaries*, s.v. "pioneer," Oxford University Press, accessed August 11, 2017, https://en.oxforddictionaries.com/definition/pioneer.

3. *Oxford English Dictionaries*, s.v. "pioneer," Oxford University Press, accessed August 11, 2017, https://en.oxforddictionaries.com/thesaurus/pioneer.

4. *Merriam-Webster*, s.v. "devotion," accessed November 16, 2017, https://www.merriam-webster.com/dictionary/devotion.

5. *Merriam-Webster*, s.v. "devotion."

6. Blue Letter Bible, s.v. *"chayil,"* accessed November 16, 2017, https://www.blueletterbible.org/lang/lexicon/lexicon.cfm?Strongs=H2428&t=KJV.

7. *Merriam-Webster*, s.v. "virtuous," accessed November 16, 2017, https://www.merriam-webster.com/dictionary/virtuous.

8. *Merriam-Webster Thesaurus*, s.v. "virtuous," accessed November 16, 2017, https://www.merriam-webster.com/thesaurus/virtuous.

Chapter 1
I Am Ruth; Hear Me Roar

1. Matthew Henry, *Matthew Henry Commentary on the Whole Bible (Concise)*, Bible Study Tools, accessed August 11, 2017, http://www.biblestudytools.com/commentaries/matthew-henry-concise/ruth/1.html. Spelling modernized for clarity.

2. *Merriam-Webster*, s.v. "destiny," accessed December 7, 2017, https://www.merriam-webster.com/dictionary/destiny.

3. 105km (username), "Lionesses on the Hunt," June 7, 2009, https://www.youtube.com/watch?v=zlJDjpe3y6I.

4. Matthew Henry, *Matthew Henry Commentary on the Whole Bible (Complete)*, Bible Study Tools, accessed August 11, 2017, http://www.biblestudytools.com/commentaries/matthew-henry -complete/ruth/1.html.

5. Henry, *Matthew Henry Commentary on the Whole Bible (Complete)*, spelling modernized for clarity.

Chapter 2
Seasons of Destiny

1. Michelle McClain-Walters, *The Deborah Anointing* (Lake Mary, FL: Charisma House, 2015), 13.

2. Matthew Henry, *Matthew Henry Commentary on the Whole Bible (Concise)*, Bible Study Tools, accessed December 11, 2017, http://www.biblestudytools.com/commentaries/matthew-henry -concise/ruth/1.html.

3. Henry, *Matthew Henry Commentary on the Whole Bible (Concise)*.

Chapter 3
Leaving the Familiar

1. *Oxford English Dictionary*, s.v. "transition," Oxford University Press, accessed August 16, 2017, https://en.oxforddictionaries.com /definition/transition.

2. *Oxford English Thesaurus*, s.v. "transition," Oxford University Press, accessed August 16, 2017, https://en.oxforddictionaries.com /thesaurus/transition.

3. Michelle McClain-Walters, *The Anna Anointing* (Lake Mary, FL: Charisma House, 2017), 111–112.

CHAPTER 4
JUST CALL ME MARA

1. Blue Letter Bible, s.v. *"marah,"* accessed August 16, 2017, https://www.blueletterbible.org/lang/lexicon/lexicon.cfm ?strongs=H4784&t=KJV.

2. John Eckhardt, *Unshakeable* (Lake Mary, FL: Charisma House, 2015), 83–84.

3. Eckhardt, *Unshakeable*, 84.

4. Matthew Henry, *Matthew Henry Commentary on the Whole Bible (Concise)*, Bible Study Tools, accessed December 15, 2017, http://www.biblestudytools.com/commentaries/matthew-henry -concise/ruth/1.html.

5. Matthew Henry, *Matthew Henry Commentary on the Whole Bible (Complete)*, Bible Study Tools, accessed December 15, http:// www.biblestudytools.com/commentaries/matthew-henry-complete /ruth/1.html.

CHAPTER 5
BORN OUT OF ADVERSITY:
GOD'S DESIGN FOR COVENANTAL CONNECTIONS

1. *Cambridge Advanced Learner's Dictionary*, s.v. "loyal," accessed August 16, 2017, https://books.google.com/books?id=PD HCFSRmjSMC&dq=isbn%3A3125179882&q=loyal#v=snippet &q=loyal&f=false.

2. *Merriam-Webster*, s.v. "covenant," accessed August 16, 2017, https://www.merriam-webster.com/dictionary/covenant.

3. Blue Letter Bible, s.v *"Ruwth,"* accessed August 16, 2017, https://www.blueletterbible.org/lang/lexicon/lexicon.cfm ?Strongs=H7327&t=KJV; Blue Letter Bible, s.v. *"re'uwth,"* accessed August 16, 2017, https://www.blueletterbible.org/lang/lexicon /lexicon.cfm?strongs=H7468&t=KJV.

4. Michelle McClain-Walters, *The Deborah Anointing* (Lake Mary, FL: Charisma House, 2015), 72–74.

CHAPTER 6
BARRIER BREAKER

1. *Merriam-Webster*, s.v. "pioneer," accessed August 17, 2017, https://www.merriam-webster.com/dictionary/pioneer.

2. *Merriam-Webster*, s.v. "barrier," accessed August 17, 2017, https://www.merriam-webster.com/dictionary/barrier.

3. Blue Letter Bible, s.v. "*Mow'ab*," accessed August 17, 2017, https://www.blueletterbible.org/lang/lexicon/lexicon.cfm?strongs=H4124.

4. Blue Letter Bible, s.v. "*Kĕmowsh*," accessed August 17, 2017, https://www.blueletterbible.org/lang/lexicon/lexicon.cfm?Strongs=H3645&t=KJV.

5. "National Snapshot: Poverty Among Women & Families, 2014," National Women's Law Center, September 17, 2015, https://nwlc.org/resources/national-snapshot-poverty-among-women-families-2014/.

6. T. D. Jakes, *Instinct* (New York: FaithWords, 2014), 32.

7. *Oxford English Dictionary*, s.v. "confidence," Oxford University Press, accessed September 1, 2017, https://en.oxforddictionaries.com/definition/us/confidence.

8. *Oxford English Thesaurus*, s.v. "confidence," Oxford University Press, accessed September 1, 2017, https://en.oxforddictionaries.com/thesaurus/confidence.

9. Katty Kay and Claire Shipman, *The Confidence Code* (New York: HarperCollins, 2014).

CHAPTER 7
A WOMAN OF VIRTUE AND EXCELLENCE

1. Blue Letter Bible, s.v. "*chayil*," accessed September 1, 2017, https://www.blueletterbible.org/lang/lexicon/lexicon.cfm?Strongs=H2428&t=KJV.

2. Blue Letter Bible, s.v. "*dynamis*," accessed September 1, 2017, https://www.blueletterbible.org/lang/lexicon/lexicon.cfm?Strongs=G1411&t=KJV.

3. The list of qualities was taken from Pat Francis, "Teaching #3 The CHAYIL Woman," accessed December 19, 2017, http://www.kingdomcovenant.ca/index.php/chayil-centre/chayil-teachings.

4. Cora Metrick-Chen, "Older Woman and Poverty," *WomanView* 19, no. 9 (March 30, 2016): 1, http://www.ncdsv.org/SSNCPL_Woman-View-Older-Women-and-Poverty_3-30-2016.pdf.

5. *Merriam-Webster*, s.v. "excellence," accessed September 6, 2017, https://www.merriam-webster.com/dictionary/excellence; *Merriam-Webster Thesaurus*, s.v. "excellence," accessed September 6, 2017, https://www.merriam-webster.com/thesaurus/excellence.

6. *Merriam-Webster*, s.v. "diligence," accessed September 5, 2017, https://www.merriam-webster.com/dictionary/diligence.

7. "Two to Get Ready—The Story of Boaz and Ruth," Bible.org, accessed September 5, 2017, https://bible.org/seriespage/5-two-get-ready-story-boaz-and-ruth.

8. *Oxford English Dictionary*, s.v. "stretch," accessed September 5, 2017, https://en.oxforddictionaries.com/definition/stretch.

CHAPTER 8
THE POWER OF REDEMPTION AND RESTORATION

1. "Two to Get Ready—The Story of Boaz and Ruth," Bible.org, accessed September 5, 2017, https://bible.org/seriespage/5-two-get-ready-story-boaz-and-ruth.

2. Blue Letter Bible, s.v. "*ga'al*," accessed September 5, 2017, https://www.blueletterbible.org/lang/lexicon/lexicon.cfm?Strongs=H1350&t=KJV.

3. Blue Letter Bible, s.v. "*duwsh*," accessed September 5, 2017, https://www.blueletterbible.org/lang/lexicon/lexicon.cfm?strongs=H1758&t=KJV.

4. "Ruth and Boaz at the Threshing Floor," *Asbury Bible Commentary*, Bible Gateway, accessed September 5, 2017, https://www.biblegateway.com/resources/asbury-bible-commentary/Ruth-Boaz-at-Threshing-Floor.

5. Blue Letter Bible, s.v. *"chacah,"* accessed November 27, 2017, https://www.blueletterbible.org/lang/lexicon/lexicon.cfm?Strongs=H2620&t=KJV.

6. Blue Letter Bible, s.v. *"No`omiy,"* accessed September 5, 2017, https://www.blueletterbible.org/lang/lexicon/lexicon.cfm?Strongs=H5281&t=KJV.